Orders: please contact Bookpoint Ltd, 130 Milton Park, Abingdon, Oxon OX14 4SB.
Telephone: (44) 01235 827720, Fax: (44) 01235 400454. Lines are open from 9.00–6.00,
Monday to Saturday, with a 24-hour message answering service.
You can also order through our website www.madaboutbooks.co.uk

British Library Cataloguing in Publication Data
A catalogue record for this title is available from The British Library

ISBN 0 340 85738 2

First published 2003
Impression number   10 9 8 7 6 5 4 3 2 1
Year 2007 2006 2005 2004 2003

Typeset by Transet Limited, Coventry, England.
Printed in Great Britain for Hodder & Stoughton Educational, a division of Hodder Headline
Plc, 338 Euston Road, London NW1 3BH by Cox & Wyman, Reading, Berks.

CONTENTS

How to use this book

The *Beginner's Guide* series aims to introduce readers to major writers of the past 500 years. It is assumed that readers will begin with little or no knowledge and will want to go on to explore the subject in other ways.

BEGIN READING THE AUTHOR

This book is a companion guide to Carter's major works; it is not a substitute for reading the books themselves. It would be useful if you read some of the works in parallel, so that you can put theory into practice. This book is divided into sections. After considering how to approach the author's work and a brief biography, we go on to explore some of the main writings and themes before examining some critical approaches to the author. The survey finishes with suggestions for further reading and possible areas of further study.

HOW TO APPROACH UNFAMILIAR OR DIFFICULT TEXTS

Coming across a new writer may seem daunting, but do not be put off. The trick is to persevere. Much good writing is multi-layered and complex. It is precisely this diversity and complexity which makes literature rewarding and exhilarating.

Literary work often needs to be read more than once and in different ways. These ways can include: a leisurely and superficial reading to get the main ideas and narrative; a slower more detailed reading focusing on the nuances of the text and on what appear to be key passages; and reading in a random way, moving back and forth through the text to examine different aspects, such as themes, narrative or characterization.

VOCABULARY

You will see that keywords and unfamiliar terms are set in **bold** text. These words are defined and explained in the Glossary to be found at the back of the book.

This book is a tool to help you appreciate a key figure in literature. We hope you enjoy reading it and find it useful.

✳ ✳ ✳ *SUMMARY* ✳ ✳ ✳

To maximize the use of this book:

- Read the author's work

- Read it several times in different ways

- Be open to innovative or unusual forms of writing

- Persevere.

Rob Abbott and Charlie Bell

Why Read Angela Carter Today?

Angela Carter is a significant figure in contemporary writing. She is a marvellous storyteller who combines the everyday realistic detail with the magical, supernatural and imaginative. Her novels, short stories and essays are topical and deal with social and political issues. They cast a new critical light on constructions and representations of power, gender and sexuality, exposing constraining social myths found in everything from fairy tales to pantomimes, Shakespeare and Renaissance paintings to popular films.

Angela Carter is arguably the most widely read contemporary woman writer in the UK today, and one of the most widely read in the USA, Australia, Europe and the Far East. Her work has been on A-level syllabuses for several years, with both *The Magic Toyshop* and *The Bloody Chamber* as popular texts for examination. Degree-level students in all contexts read, enjoy and study her work.

Lesser known texts such as the early *Fireworks* have been brought out in paperback, short stories are collected in *Burning your Boats*, dramas in *Come Unto These Yellow Sands*, and critical essays in *Expletives Deleted*. Her work is read alongside that of other contemporary postmodernists such as Ian McEwan and Will Self, contemporary women writers such as Fay Weldon, radical and feminist writers perceptive about issues and representations of race, class, gender and power such as Toni Morrison, and magic realists such as Gabriel Garcia Marquez. Individual works such as *The Magic Toyshop* and 'The Company of Wolves' have been made into successful films.

A RADICAL WRITER

Angela Carter is a radical contemporary writer whose work could be described as both feminist and postmodernist (though she did not use the terms of herself).

I believe that all myths are products of the human mind and reflect only aspects of material human practice. I'm in the demythologising business ...

('Notes from the Front Line', in *On Gender and Writing*,
1984, pp.70, 71)

This expression of interest in exploring and exposing constructions of femininity which have been a crucial, contested part of women's social make-up clearly places Angela Carter as a feminist writer. Carter equally critiques versions of masculinity. She aims to expose the social and cultural myths which condition and control us all. In so doing, she adopts, then adapts and critiques the content and form of many of these myths, rewriting fairy tales ('The Bloody Chamber') plays, films ('John Ford's "T'is Pity She's a Whore"'), pantomimes ('In Pantoland') and other popular cultural expressions of myths.

USE OF POPULAR FORMS

Angela Carter uses the imagery, language and the forms of popular genres in her work. She is in touch with the lives and imaginations of ordinary people. Established traditional myths, archetypes reproduced and continued through literature and art, contemporary social mythology, and popular genres from romantic fiction to music hall are the raw materials from which she constructs character, narrative and incident. *The Magic Toyshop* reworks stories found in girls' magazines, 'Cinderella', and versions of woman and of pornography and power found in literature and art. A further and more thorough analysis of the formations of sexualized power found in modern society appears in *The Sadeian Woman*, a work of argument which, in providing a reinterpretation of the Marquis de Sade, exposes the dubious base of society's delight in Hollywood figures such as Marilyn Monroe. Idealizing women is revealed as including involving their taking a secondary role. Woman's conformity to this idealization and to male-defined roles is seen as collusion. Carter looks again at female sexuality, and power.

Carter picks her words carefully and ensures everything signifies, indicating choices made by people and for people. Foregrounding and exaggeration expose the influences of dominant benefits or ideology. Horror and the comic, carnivalesque reversals, show both worst case scenarios such as women as puppets (*The Magic Toyshop*, 'The Loves of Lady Purple'), and romantic love as vampiric and deadly ('Lady in the House of Love'). Carter also suggests alternatives: men and women as newly fledged equals (*Nights at the Circus*), and the power of the imaginative life and of close relationships to overcome the decay and sterility of age (*Wise Children*). Carter's work has designs upon us, messages about social equality and human potential. Her stories and characters are lively, entertaining, powerful and, frequently, very funny.

STYLE

Carter combines both historically realistic description and fantasy, the world of the imagination, the rich evocation of metaphor. This she does to explore the everyday world of specific periods such as the nineteenth century in London and abroad (*Nights at the Circus*) when women's freedoms are about to flourish; post-Second World War in London (*Wise Children*) with austerity and music hall, and the world of the inner imagination, no less real. This latter is accomplished through using fantasy, metaphor, Gothic, horror, science fiction, and the form combining all of these, **magic realism**.

Angela Carter's elaborate style is a surprise for readers expecting realist prose, or straight argument providing political and sexual message. *New Society* contributions and witty, perceptive essays in *Nothing Sacred* can seem to sit uneasily beside the

KEYWORD

Magic realism: originating in the works of Latin American writers such as Gabriel Garcia Marquez from the 1960s onwards, magic realism is a form of writing combining both the factual or realistic, and the magical, imaginative and supernatural. Authors show people's imaginative, lived feelings *and* what they actually say and do. It enables writers to show paradox, contradictions. Great twentieth-century magic realists include Angela Carter and Toni Morrison.

reworking of fairy tales. But each provide witty, perceptive comments on, and alternatives to, the deceptions and constraints which are cultural representations of gendered roles for men and women in high art, popular cultural mythology and the everyday world.

Laced with adjectives and metaphors, her style is a successful vehicle for analysis of the prison house of ideology or beliefs as well as of language. Her language is rich with comparisons, similes, metaphors and with paradox. Her favourite term is the **oxymoron**.

KEYWORD

Oxymoron: a conjunction of contradictions, of opposites, such as 'beautiful decay' 'exquisite corpse' and it shows up contradictions, what is hidden.

Carter's use of the oxymoron combines the imaginative and the everyday, linking sex and death, life and death, beauty and the acceptable, in contrast to the rejection of what is considered other or different. Both beauty (ideal) and the other (not me, something different and so frightening) are seen as social constructions. The oxymoron is a figure familiar to readers of the Gothic, and Carter is a Gothic writer who combines opposites to expose the desires and fears hidden beneath the seemingly calm, conformist surface of the world around us, families, our sense of identity and continuity, of right and wrong. Carter uses Gothic settings, language and its paradoxes to expose social contradictions and the oppressions of socially constructed myths about gender and power relations which affect the ways we see ourselves in something.

* * *SUMMARY* * *

- Angela Carter is a significant figure in contemporary writing, and in women's writing; feminist and postmodernist in style and concerns.

- She is a marvellous storyteller, combining everyday realistic detail with the magical, supernatural and imaginative.

- Her novels, short stories and essays are topical and engaged, casting new critical light on constructions and representations of power, gender and sexuality, exposing constraining social myths.

- She uses myths, fairy tales, and popular fictional forms to represent and critique the world around us.

- Her style is excessive, elaborate. Filled with paradox, making use of both horror and humour, it uses elements of the Gothic to critique social constructions and suggest alternatives.

How to Approach Angela Carter

We can read Angela Carter's work as both entertaining and a critique of constructions and representations of power, gender, sexuality and cultural difference. Discussion and reading of extracts from her short story 'The Company of Wolves' and close reading of the introduction to *The Magic Toyshop* emphasizes Carter's fascinating mixture of the everyday realistic with myths, the supernatural and the magical. Carter uses a variety of writing strategies such as magic realism, horror, irony and farce. Her language is rich with paradox, imagery and symbol, highlighting contradictions and constraints, offering alternative celebratory examples and ways of seeing the world, of identity, relations and of power.

Reading a new Angela Carter novel resembles the initial experience of the wife in 'The Bloody Chamber'. As we read, we unlock hidden horrors and surprises. Most particularly, there are revelations about oppressive power relations and gendered inequalities. Everything, every line, name and metaphor are so packed with meaning that we are almost overwhelmed with all we find. Feminist and other criticism often fails to recognize the humour and the refusal to provide an ideal resolution in Carter's work. Solutions and denouements are ironic; she does not substitute alternative myths for those she has deconstructed.

Embellished, resonant with ambiguity and reference, her style is a successful vehicle for analysis and exposé of cultural myths, social constructions. Angela Carter's writing is rich and lively. She is an accomplished storyteller, both timeless and topical in her concerns. Engaged with the ways language and forms of power constrain or enable people, Carter reveals paradoxes and contradictions, undercutting society's destructive, dangerous constructions of some people (women, children, foreigners) as **'other'**, to be restrained, misunderstood and silenced.

Let us look at a typical piece of Carter's writing, concentrating on the quality of her writing, its imagery and references, the storytelling and use of the comic and the critical, and its specific focus on critiquing representations of gender and power.

KEYWORD

Other: a critical term used in much post-colonial and horror writing. It suggests the emphasis of difference, foreignness, leading to prejudice and oppression.

OPENING OF *THE MAGIC TOYSHOP*

In the opening pages of *The Magic Toyshop* Angela Carter focuses on teenager Melanie. She explores the ways in which women and girls construct versions of themselves and their gendered identities, influenced by representations from high art (both painting and literature produced by men) and popular culture – particularly girls' books and Hollywood films. These versions, she suggests, constrain women's self-development and often place them in subordinate roles, hidden, silenced, conned by various romantic myths and ideals. Melanie, just turned 15, explores her own changing body, surprised at it.

On came the swan, its feet going 'splat', 'splat', 'splat'

She 'discovered she was made of flesh and blood'. Initially, she only uses the images and language of male artists and writers in her exploration. Angela Carter frequently uses **intertextuality**, other writing by other writers, references to and quotations from art and film.

Here Carter uses John Donne, the seventeenth-century poet who wrote a variety of poems, particularly sonnets, about his love for his mistresses. 'O My America, my new found land' suggests that Melanie is discovering her own body but through the male gaze, the eyes of male discoverers, first Donne, through his poetry and then the explorers Mungo Park, Cortez and da Gama. Melanie, however, begins turning cartwheels and doing handstands, reclaiming her own body in her own way, and showing herself to be a child as much as a growing woman. Melanie, it is suggested, will not necessarily end up constrained by traditional versions of what women are expected to be because she has such energy and control of her own body. However, she next starts to pose in front of the mirror in attitudes and with accessories each recalling the portrayal of women by a variety of male artists. She poses as a **pre-Raphaelite** ideal woman.

KEYWORDS

Intertextuality: used by artists and writers of all kinds, particularly twentieth- and twenty-first-century writers, intertextuality is the deliberate referencing, direct use of, mingling into a work of other works by other artists and writers suggesting their influence, contradictions or parallels with their arguments and ideas.

Pre-Raphaelite: the pre-Raphaelite Brotherhood was a group of mid-nineteenth-century writers and artists, including Dante Gabriel Rossetti and Holman Hunt. They revived the very realistic styles of painting that were popular before the work of the Renaissance painter Raphael, and did so to tell stories, retell myths and comment socially on everything from moral laxity to emigration.

Next Melanie poses as a model for the nineteenth-century French painter Toulouse Lautrec (who painted prostitutes) and the Renaissance painter Cranach who painted rather skinny images of Adam and Eve. This scene reminds readers of the moments in their own lives when they try on different roles and versions of sexuality and identity. Many readers will have tried to compose versions of themselves based on contemporary singers or models, and will probably have found their own bodies rather un-idealized, as does Melanie. She is too thin for one version of woman, too fat for another and so on. Carter suggests that women try fitting versions and images of their selves and their sexuality into those portrayed by male artists and writers, while their very bodily and personal differences refuse such constraints.

Carter's particular talent is to make the complex accessible and amusing. The reader does not need to know the references, although this helps enrich reading, because she explains what each reference suggests, that Melanie's body is depicted by others but she is trying on versions of her growing self, and that she finds it difficult to fit into these imposed versions. The passage is funny, very accessible. It is like our own lives, and also critical of high-art constructions and representations of women constraining women's versions of themselves and their sexuality. In its criticism, it indicts the destructive effects of the oppressive power of **patriarchy**, exposing how art and myths of all kinds collude with beliefs and behaviours legitimized by such power.

KEYWORD

Patriarchy: this literally means the law of the father, but has been taken to suggest legitimized, enforced, male dominated oppression. Many feminist thinkers such as writer Virginia Woolf, or French feminist theorist Hélène Cixous, have written against the damage that patriarchal power has done to women, and to the vulnerable (children, people from other countries, the poor), subordinating and silencing them. It is important to note that criticizing patriarchy is not a criticism of men as such but of oppressive power enabled by a damaging male dominance.

The passage becomes increasingly amusing. Melanie reads read *Lady Chatterley's Lover* by D.H. Lawrence, an early twentieth-century text which portrayed sexuality and sexual relations in a very revealing and unconventional way but, nonetheless, depicted women as always longing for the sexual power imposed by men. Melanie then 'secretly picked forget-me-nots and stuck them in her pubic hair'. This is what Connie Chatterley does in her relationship with Mellors, the gamekeeper in Lawrence's novel, so Melanie copies literary characters, but Carter also satirizes this scene. It is funny, silly, inappropriate. Melanie constructs versions of herself based on Hollywood movies of the 1950s (romantic comedies, typically starring Doris Day or Marilyn Monroe) indicating to the reader that she imagines the height of maturity as marriage, but has no idea of the subsequent sexual relations or domesticity. She is shown as rather naive, unaware of sex and of the housewife role. 'She gift-wrapped herself for a phantom bridegroom cleaning his teeth in honeymoon Cannes or Nice or Miami Beach.' This bridegroom is cleaning his teeth. All Melanie can imagine about couples married and going to bed is that they will clean their teeth. She has obtained this view from Hollywood movies which refused to depict sex, but she is also aware that she must be attractive and must pose for this pretend bridegroom, and so checks out her body, revealing bits of thigh. Like most young women, she finds her body does not quite match up to the movie ideal, but it is very much her own: young, lively, changing.

The scene is amusing, but Carter also indicates problems, potential constraints and potential abuse which could follow buying into such artificial images of what women 'should be' in relation to men. Melanie's pyjamas are contained in a pyjama case resembling Edward Bear. This casts her as a child, but also indicates potential pregnancy; the bear's stomach is swollen. Melanie has been reading the children's classic *Lorna Doone*. The book is interesting yet dangerous, dealing in relationships, power and potential abuse. Lorna Doone's kidnapping is actually more threatening than entertaining. The book is 'splayed face down in the dust under the bed', both a conventional spot for us to put down our books when reading in bed, and suggestive of rape. Carter is realistic and critical in such descriptions in order to engage with ordinary people both to represent their lives and to critique high art, popular culture, films and children's books, showing them as vehicles for constructing and constraining people in gender and power inflected roles.

The novel exposes gender stereotyping and fictional representations of this in high art, popular fiction, mythology, girls'/women's books and stories. Angela Carter uses all the clichés. Melanie's parents die in an air crash, leaving her orphaned, a 'little mother' to her siblings, lodging with a wicked uncle. Uncle Philip is the archetypal patriarch, and Aunt Margaret embodies the logical results of total male dominance; she is dumb.

'THE COMPANY OF WOLVES'

Many of Carter's short stories rewrite traditional fairy tales and myths in order to deconstruct them, revealing the meanings and intentions they have upon us, the morals and behaviours they teach, ways in which they represent life and values. In rewriting a number of fairy tales, myths and legends ranging from 'Beauty and the Beast' ('The Courtship of Mr Lyon') to tales about the violence and threat of werewolves ('Company Of Wolves', 'Wolf Alice', 'The Were-Wolf') Carter encourages us to look anew at what the tales do, or do not, reveal about power and representation, and to see that other behaviours are possible. This is dramatized through alternative options made available in the rewritten tales, opened up by revealing each tale as only that, a story, a fiction, a construct with designs upon us. 'The Company of Wolves' is a rewritten version of 'Little Red Riding Hood', one emphasizing sexual danger, controls, threats and the claiming of sexual energy and identity.

In 'The Company of Wolves', the yoking of opposites in language, techniques and descriptions, enact the attraction and terror of what could seem comfortably relegated to nightmare and myth, but is immediate in its assault on our senses:

> At night the eyes of wolves shine like candle flames, yellowish, reddish, but that is because the pupils of their eyes fatten on darkness and catch the light from your lantern to flash it back to you – red for danger; if a wolf's eyes reflect only moonlight, then they gleam a cold and unnatural green, a mineral, a piercing colour. If the benighted traveller spies those

luminous, terrible sequins stitched suddenly on the black thickets, then
he knows he must run, if fear has not struck him stock-still.

                                                                (1996, p.212).

She starts with the familiar, involving us directly, 'you', before moving
sharply into the realm of cold, hard difference; beauty and pain,
attraction and repulsion. We are seduced by the 'luminous, terrible
sequins', simultaneously attracted and repulsed. Benighted travellers,
Carter insists we must run but cannot. This is the terrifying stasis of
nightmare. Much of Carter's writing uses the strategies of nightmare
and horror to both entertain and critique social constructions of
power. 'Fatten' reminds us that wolves long to devour us. The flashing
of lantern to eye indicates a close, inevitable relation between traveller
and wolf.

Carter's language details monstrous shape-changing and limb-ripping,
forest terrors and cannibalism. By directly addressing the monstrous,
she shows us not only that horror is disturbingly close, but that we
produce it; it is our emerging dark side which must be acknowledged.

Werewolves lurk in several of Angela Carter's short stories. Borderline
creatures of the night, they remind us of our animal natures, celebrants
of violent forces held at bay by the trappings of humanity. Werewolves,
along with vampires, haunt the popular cultural imaginary. Both beast
and human, werewolves cross the threshold between the familiar and
the terrifying other. Even when you feel comfortable and safe, 'the
wolves have ways of arriving at your own hearthside'. You might
conform to the expectations of civilized society, believing that 'We keep
the wolves outside by living well', (p.213) but these dangerous creatures
cross all thresholds, enter the marriage bed, the kitchen, granny's
bedroom and the people we know because, 'The worst wolves are hairy
on the inside.' Werewolves represent our own animal natures which we
try to ignore and keep at bay. Those hiding their brutality under a
civilized veneer are most to be feared. In Carter's rewritten version of
'Little Red Riding Hood' the young girl has no intention of being

She knew she was nobody's meat

devoured like her granny. She recognizes both the humanity and the otherness, the danger and the seductive attraction of the wolf, replays the exchanges of the fairy tale ('what big teeth you have' and so on), throws their clothes into the fire and leaps into bed with the wolf, pacifying him.

✳ ✳ ✳ *SUMMARY* ✳ ✳ ✳

Angela Carter's writing:

● explores and critiques representations of relationships of gender and power, of sexuality, as portrayed in high art, popular culture, fairy tales, myths and the world around us.

● focuses on relationships and individual development within the family, on adolescence, maturity and old age.

● cuts through beliefs and practices which cast some people as 'other', as victims, monsters and freaks, using the reversals and celebrations of the 'carnival' to embody alternatives.

● uses intertextuality, black humour, fragmentation, irony and horror.

● uses 'magic realism': a mixture of the historical/real with the imaginative/mythic, mixing complex symbolic imagery and beautifully written prose, labyrinthine plots and popular fictional formulae, comedy and horror in critique and celebration.

3 Angela Carter, 1940–92: Biography and Influences

Born Angela Olive Stalker on 7 May in wartime Eastbourne, Sussex, in 1940, Angela Carter was brought up during the war in Yorkshire with her maternal grandmother in a household dominated by women. When the war ended she moved to South London and was educated in Balham, a lower middle-class area into which more affluent people have moved latterly. She has one brother. Angela Carter's upbringing and teenage years in 1950s London re-emerge in settings for *The Magic Toyshop* and *Wise Children*. The earlier novel has Melanie and her brother and sister living above a toyshop in a Dickensian street, while in *Wise Children* the elderly 'hoofers' or music hall performers and dancers, Dora and Nora Chance, live in a house inherited from their grandmother. As a child and adolescent, Carter was an avid film goer and her father would take her to the old Hollywood films in the (then) glamorized elegance and opulent settings of local cinemas, where she was influenced by the artifice, the excess and the glamorous representations of men and women, particularly that of various screen goddesses. Her appreciation of artifice and elegance influenced her lifelong love of the cinema and Hollywood film, and her awareness of how gender and identity are social constructions. This directly affected her portrayal, in *The Passion of New Eve*, of Tristessa, the transvestite screen goddess who represents both the constructedness of gender roles and the vulnerability of individuals. This delicately maintained artifice is echoed in her/his brittle, easily destroyed house. Hollywood film also re-emerges in the making of the grand 1940s' epic film version of Shakespeare's *A Midsummer Night's Dream*, which provides a chaotic centrepiece for *Wise Children*.

Angela Carter worked for some time as a junior reporter on the *Croydon Advertiser*, where she probably gained insights into human nature and the everyday world. She read English at Bristol 1962–65. Divorcing her first husband, she went to live in Japan from 1969 to 1972 where she said she felt huge and ungainly, oddly foreign. But this experience of estrangement affected her writing about the constructs of gender roles, the representation of self and her awareness of the multiple possibilities of identity and reality. 'Flesh and the Mirror', a short story about a chance sexual encounter in Japan, explores ways in which reflections of self and other help construct dramatized versions of self, depict a bodily self outside the thinking mind. This sense of artifice, construction and role-play dominates her writing of this period, and afterwards. Explicitly about a sexual encounter with a stranger, this tale also acts as a model for her lively sexual explorations and critiques questioning established and received views about sexual relations. These range from the brothel of *Nights at the Circus*; the exploration of unbalanced freedoms (men with money have sexual freedom; women without it only *seem* to have freedom) in *The Sadeian Woman*, and explorations of alternative forms of sexual and caring relationships in *Nights at the Circus* (with Walser the journalist), and 'The Bloody Chamber' (with the blind piano-tuner).

Her writing has won her several awards: the John Lewellyn Rhys prize for *The Magic Toyshop*, 1967; Somerset Maugham award for *Several Perceptions*, 1968, and the James Tait Black memorial prize for *Nights at the Circus*, 1985. Alongside writing, she travelled and taught, at Brown University, Rhode Island, USA, 1980–81; at the University of East Anglia on the creative writing MA, 1984–87; the University of Adelaide, 1984; Austin Texas, 1985; Iowa City, 1986; Albany, New York State, 1988. This travel infiltrates her work, her fascination with Hollywood (*Passion of New Eve, Wise Children*) and with the USA in general (*American Ghosts* and *Old World Wonders*).

THE GOTHIC INFLUENCES

I'd always been fond of Poe, and Hoffmann—Gothic tales, cruel tales, tales of wonder, tales of terror, fabulous narratives that deal directly with the imagery of the unconscious–mirrors; the externalized self; forsaken castles; haunted forests; forbidden sexual objects.

(Afterword to *Fireworks*, 1974, pp.132–3)

Some of Carter's short stories and essays explore the influences of horror writer Edgar Allan Poe, by Shakespeare, Yeats and many modernist and nineteenth-century writers, by popular Hollywood films, pantomimes and fairy tales, and by the writings of the Marquis de Sade. This rich mixture and her baroque, embellished style, her breadth of textual, mythical and media reference, and her fascination with paradox, make hers an insightful, wry critical voice.

Carter's penchant for the **Gothic** and horror also springs from nineteenth-century writing, from *Jane Eyre* with its madwoman in the attic, representation of Jane's restrained, repressed sexuality, with dungeons and attics, winding stairs, Gothic locations, and with the formulae of the Gothic – twinning, alternatives, mirroring. Gothic tales provide opportunities for social critique. Through the ostensibly sound surface of society creep and leak contradictions and alternatives which undercut that neat surface. These contradictions provide an opportunity to analyse and criticize relationships of power and money affecting gender, identity, and the way people live their lives. Carter, an exponent of the **contemporary feminist Gothic**, critiques representations of roles for women, and men. She also utilizes the

KEYWORD

Gothic and contemporary feminist Gothic: Gothic is a term linked to gothic architecture, soaring turrets, dungeons, winding stairs, and buildings. But in literary terms the Gothic is usually seen to begin with Horace Walpole's *Castle of Otranto* and Anne Radcliffe's *Mysteries of Udolpho*. It forms a major influence in much nineteenth-century writing, particularly romantic tales which also involve incarceration, threats, virginity and tyrannical, powerful men. Gothic also was used as a vehicle for social critique. Ostensibly secure social situations – families, relationships, homes, – are seen as founded on doubt and deception, their contradictions leak through in imagery of gap and breaks, mirrors and contradictions. In conventional nineteenth-century Gothic, usually such exposés of contradiction lead to a final, secure ending with order restored. In contemporary feminist Gothic, the very kind of security and stability is cast in doubt, seen as reinforcing an order more supportive of dominant middle-class white masculinist beliefs and behaviours, and not so generously inclined towards the needs and lives of women. So some contemporary Gothic writers, such as Michele Roberts and Angela Carter, refuse neat endings and the restoration of order.

literary strategies of horror, a more terrifying and violent Gothic form, and so shows the potential for extreme nastiness, oppression and even death lurking beneath social norms and everyday relationships. In 'The Fall Rivers Axe Murders' Carter uses both horror strategies and a famous shocking tale of the murder of a whole family by the daughter, Lizzie Borden. Lizzie is driven out of control because of the hothouse, oppressive Puritan atmosphere in small town Fall Rivers. The silencing and the incarceration she suffers in a house more a monument to death (her father is an undertaker, in a strait-laced, hypocritical society) triggers a fatal response. Lizzie breaks out as an axe murderer. The tale shows the influence of Poe who also explored hypocrisy, incarceration, lies and deceit, relationships of power and the return of the repressed. Carter's own horror and Gothic tales include figures of vampires, werewolves, ghosts, demon lovers and sadistic behaviour. She frequently explores the danger and violence on and by women, and frequently re-empowers women at the tale's end. In 'The Loves of Lady Purple', a puppet comes to life, refuses the scenes she has been constructed to play, drains her master and walks off into town to establish herself in a brothel.

FEMINISM

Scrutiny of gender-based inequalities and arguments for the re-empowerment of women became popular in the late 1960s onwards with the development of **second-wave feminism**, and Angela Carter although not calling herself a feminist, can be seen as aligned with the values, beliefs and behaviours of the Women's Movement.

KEYWORD

Second-wave feminism: second-wave feminism, or the Women's Movement, started in the late 1960s with demands for equal rights and equal pay. Some writers and thinkers rediscovered goddess myths, imagining matriarchal communities which would refuse war, and violence, (seen as largely male activities). 'Take back the night' marches insisted that women should be free to live their own lives, not preyed on by the violence of men in the night streets. The movement, articulated in 1970's texts such as Germaine Greer's *The Female Eunuch* and Kate Millet's *Sexual Politics*, heralded a sexual revolution and led to changes in the material, legal and social situation of many women.

Carter took up and dramatized arguments of sexual equality and celebration of women's sexual energies in her lively tales of powerful women including, among others, Fevvers the Cockney Venus, winged aerialiste (*Nights at the Circus*); her new version of Little Red Riding Hood who seizes her sexuality, jumping into the arms of the wolf in granny's bed ('The Company of Wolves') and Nora and Dora Chance, twin music hall performers whose sexual exploits run throughout *Wise Children*. She also scrutinizes and attacks relationships of oppression and power through images such as the silence of Aunt Margaret with her choker (*The Magic Toyshop*), and the bizarre fetishist fascination with silenced, sleeping and near dead women in Madame Schreck's brothel (*Nights at the Circus*).

PERFORMANCE

Angela Carter was also influenced by Shakespeare, Yeats and many modernist and nineteenth-century writers, by popular Hollywood films, pantomimes and fairy tales. She exposes the underlying beliefs of these works, intervening on them and on Hollywood film, pantomime, popular fictions and fairy tales, to explore and rewrite cultural myths. In, 'In Pantoland' she plays with pantomime's gender cross-dressing: principal boys played by girls, dames by men. This work exposes pantomime as an extreme example of ways in which all social constructions of gender are just that, constructions, representations which people copy and obey, but which could restrict individuality and their identities. The subversive, comic energies of the pantomime are a model for her own challenges to culture and social constraints, which emerge in her use of the forms of **carnival**.

KEYWORD

Carnival: the critical term 'carnival' was coined by Mikhail Bakhtin, who recognized that in medieval and Renaissance days, ordinary people would, on certain days of the year, particularly Twelfth Night and midsummer, turn the tables, mock the rich, play, celebrate and have fun. Bakhtin labelled these activities and other subversive, energetic critiques as 'carnival', now a term used by many contemporary writers, creative and critical, to identify reactions against repression, the celebratory energies of alternative ways of living, something of a lively riotous time.

Carter uses Shakespeare's *A Midsummer Night's Dream* in *Wise Children*. Its excess and disorder are an opportunity for the social tables to be turned, love in the bushes, mistaken identity and much fun. She celebrates the subversive energies of women, (Fevvers in *Nights at the Circus*), those controlled by others as if puppets ('The Loves of Lady Purple') and the working classes.

Her own statement 'I'm in the demythologizing business', emphasizes ways in which she sets out to expose the damage done by constraints of myths of gender roles in particular, a contribution which influenced many contemporary writers, male and female, from Ian McEwan to Pat Barker. Carter is influenced by and has influenced feminist thought and critical practice, and her work has made a substantial contribution to postmodernist writing.

✳ ✳ ✳ *SUMMARY* ✳ ✳ ✳

● Angela Carter's background in post-war lower middle-class London informs several works.

● Her influences are from fairy tale, myth, horror and popular film as well as high art and the literary 'canon' including Shakespeare, Poe and Yeats.

● Her work comprises publishing, teaching, travel and critical reputation.

● She has been influenced by and has had influence on feminist thought and critical practice.

● She uses the carnivalesque for critique, celebration, suggestions of other ways of living.

4 Major Themes

Carter was acutely observant of the world around her. Her sense of the historical and cultural differences of, for instance, turn of the century Russia, nineteenth-century England, the 1960s swinging London, late twentieth-century Japan, are rarely drawn in straightforward, realistic, historical detail. Instead, she mixes the realistic with the imaginative, fantastic and magical, and in so doing she enables imaginative insights to cast a spotlight on people, places, behaviours and beliefs, to ironize, analyse, criticize and sometimes to suggest that things and people could behave otherwise. She is a writer with designs upon us, but these are never obvious prescriptions; instead she works by allusion, comedy, horror, satire, using the mythical, both contemporary cultural myth and the established myth of traditional high art, Renaissance painting and canonical texts, and lower art of the people, including fairy tale.

Angela Carter was, among much else, an early contributor to a popular feminist onslaught on the conventions of myths, fairy tales, popular films and horror writing. As such, she addressed genres dominated by male practitioners, and by male fears of both female sexuality and female subjectivity. Her work uses fantasy, horror and humour to critique sexualized power relations and stereotypes of women, and men. Her transformations of fairy tales are culturally critical. Rereading the tales of monsters and golden-haired heroines, she refuses their often conservative meanings, exposing their subtexts. The same is true of reading film. In popular Hollywood film, women are idealized, doll-like and manipulated, agents and products of an entertaining but false and constraining fantasy world (exposed in *The Passion of New Eve*). Men in Carter's work are often revealed, not as romantic heroes, strong and dependable fathers, ideal lovers, but as bullies, domineering tyrants and insensitive, often sadistic, partners.

GENDER, PERFORMANCE AND CONSTRUCTION

Influenced by writers such as Judith Butler and Michel Foucault, Carter argues (in *The Sadeian Woman* and essays) and dramatizes (in *Nights at the Circus* and *The Passion of New Eve*) her awareness, popular amongst postmodernist writers (such as Martin Amis, John Hawkes, Thomas Pynchon and Fay Weldon), that gender is performance, construction and artifice in film and all forms of popular entertainment, and played out in everyday life. Carter explores and exposes this, emphasizing its dangers because it can restrain people and limit their sense of identity, their ability to change. She also shows its potential for carnival and celebration, fun, reversals of power and the development of alternative versions of self and relationships. When we realize that gendered roles are social constructions rather than natural, as is biology, we can see how some use these roles to constrain others, but we can also see how we may choose different roles, and behave differently. This awareness is liberating and potentially creative.

Carter's fascination with the stage and film, with advertisements and all forms of popular culture, reveals how we present ourselves to ourselves, and ourselves to others. She makes good use of the popular fictional forms which most regularly, and explicitly, enact conventional beliefs of popular culture. In so doing, she also critiques the structures and world views offered by such popular fictional forms, specifically horror, romantic fiction and science fiction.

MYTHS – POPULAR, CULTURAL AND HISTORICAL – DEMYTHOLOGIZED

Reclaiming and redefining of myths, symbols, legends, fairy tales, the culturally produced forms which underlie our visions of ourselves as women and men, is one major way in which Angela Carter subverts culturally conditioned gender inequalities. She transforms fairy tales, rereading the gendered scripts of monsters and golden-haired heroines, refusing the often implicit conservative meanings, exposing how they support social and sexual power relations. Carter exposes, plays with and demythologizes myths which construct and constrain lives. In her early work she rewrites conventional fairy tales such as those of the Brothers Grimm and Perrault, exposing their latent sexism.

In rewriting the Bluebeard myth (also a favourite of Margaret Atwood's) in 'The Bloody Chamber', Carter exposes the dangerous sado-masochistic mutual attraction of a young impoverished girl for an older, wealthy man, Marquis and art connoisseur, who offers her a seemingly caring relationship which is actually a front for tyranny.

The Marquis selects his new wife as commodity, ornament and feast for the eyes to be owned and devoured.

> Rapt, he intoned: 'Of her apparel she retains only her sonorous jewellery'
> ... A dozen husbands impaled a dozen brides while the mewing gulls
> swung on invisible trapezes in the empty air outside.
>
> (p.121)

Threats of violence attract and repel the new bride, recognizing his 'connoisseur's look' inspecting her like so much meat on a slab. But she is overwhelmed by his attention and the undying love offered. She is poor, with few job opportunities, is flattered by his gifts, wooing, financial security, the trappings of romantic fiction. To him, however, she is an object both beautiful and to be literally consumed. The monstrous Bluebeard husband figuratively devours his bride as he disempowers and sexually ravishes her, attempting also to control her imagination and quest for knowledge. Later, in *The Sadeian Woman* (1979) Carter explores literal consuming passions; connections between sexual oppression, cannibalism and horror.

On his temporary departure, the Marquis hands her the keys, impressing on her the role as mistress of the castle, telling her she has free run, but must not open one specific room. Of course she opens it. Inside she finds the bodies of his previous wives, a fate which, she then realizes, awaits her. Upon his return, he intends to slaughter this new wife because of her challenge to his power, her seeking after knowledge. In the traditional tale, she is rescued by her brothers. In Carter's version, her mother comes to the rescue, a warrior figure, chivalric, powerful, she storms the castle. The girl settles down with a blind piano-tuner, her support during her ordeal.

CRITIQUING GENDER REPRESENTATIONS

Other stories by Angela Carter critique the infantalizing and disempowering image of women, as the 'Living Doll' of popular culture and myth. She exposes myths which underlie sexual stereotyping and oppressive behaviours perpetuated by high art and popular culture. These are, mainly, myths depicting women as sexual objects, possessions, necessarily victims, naturally silent, powerless and hesitant. Carter exposes behind such representations, conventional male fears of women's potential for individuality, sexual and other choices, energy, the right to say and do things differently. In so doing, Carter uses theories underlying feminist critics' exposure of limited representations of women in popular culture, myth and high art, underpinned by law, religion and literature. She uses the theories of Michael Foucault, and the post-Freudian French feminists: Hélène Cixous, Luce Irigaray and Julia Kristeva. A feminist reading position is constructed, renegotiating relationships of power. By exposing representations as mere changeable constructions, she produces writing which is liberating, exciting and usually amusing, dealing ironically with conventional versions. So high-art representations of women are challenged in Melanie's youthful development of identity in *The Magic Toyshop*; Fevvers in *Nights at the Circus* refuses various patriarchal power games to turn her into a myth (with Christian Rosencreutz) to be sacrificed, or a doll (with the Grand Duke), and Dora and Nora Chance play to and so rather send up the audience's versions of good time female music hall 'hoofers' in *Wise Children*.

USE OF MAGIC REALISM

Angela Carter uses the strategies of magic realism to examine and explore ways in which we see and express our experiences, both the everyday, real historical moments of events, shared realities, visible and notable happenings, and the feelings, our dreams and fears, the workings of our imaginations, the spiritual, magical and supernatural. The historical, the everyday real produced by Carter could include, for example political moments, and the texture of historical moments and places such as Second World War boarding houses – both in *Wise Children*.

George Lukacs, a Marxist historical critic, identifies ways in which we construct and represent historical and realistic contexts and experiences. He points out that writers choose well-known dates and places – London, Paris, the end of the war – then select items of furniture, clothing, popular culture, indicating the texture and paraphernalia of the moment. A fictional ploy, it nonetheless gives the reader a sense of the solidly shared real. However, the inner thoughts, feelings, dreams, fears and imaginations of people are always also experienced and lived at any moment, and writers such as Toni Morrison and Angela Carter re-create these for us using the magical, the supernatural and the spiritual (more frequently found in Morrison), and the mythical, the fairy tale and the symbolic (more frequently found in Carter).

In *The Magic Toyshop* Angela Carter investigates and ironizes ways in which adolescent girls develop a sense of their gendered identity culturally based in male imaged popular and high art.

Melanie can only imagine marriage as her future. One night she decides to try on her mother's wedding dress. Wrestling with a dress too loose and alien for her body, she is almost overwhelmed. Escaping into the garden to play, she is trapped: the front door slams behind her. In order to return to her room to make amends, she climbs the apple 'tree of knowledge' out of her own first Eden garden, but rips the dress.

Subsequently, she blames herself for the deaths of her parents in an air crash. Carter's pastiche, her intertextual use of myth, image, symbol, literary, artistic and popular cultural representation in this realistic/Gothic tale confronts the reader with a tightly woven web of links and relations. We perceive at every turn how high and popular culture continually reinforce certain myths of subordination and oppression, both gender and race/religion related. Queen Victoria is seen as a broken statue in Finn's favourite garden, and the Irish Jowle family are oppressed in Uncle Philip's household. Myths are inscribed in everyday reality.

A carnivalesque, celebratory remythologizing takes place in both *Nights at the Circus* and *Wise Children*, Angela Carter's final novels. While *Wise Children* deals directly with the central issues of the relationship between reason and imagination, logic and magic, in a reinterpretation of *A Midsummer Night's Dream*, *Nights at the Circus* flies in the face of patriarchy, or oppressive male power.

As a Cockney Venus, Fevvers is the embodiment of several realized myths, not least that of the East End whore with a heart of gold, as well as that of the delicate, caged bird/woman and ship's figurehead. She is a fusion of man's uneasy, contradictory versions of woman. Leda and the Swan, used in *The Magic Toyshop*, re-emerges alongside other myths. Capitalist power structures entice as well as entrap Fevvers. Painted white, she poses as icon of chastity and femininity in Ma Nelson's whorehouse, moving on to help re-enact different, more perverse male sexual fantasies fuelled by de Sade, in the Gothic dungeons of Madame Schreck's brothel where Fevvers is one of the *tableaux vivants* of women in the 'profane altars' at which punters come to worship. Myth, symbol, power and cash are recalled in the reference to Yeats's 'The Circus Animals' Desertion' this 'lumber room of femininity, this rag and bone shop of the heart' (1984, p.49).

It is specifically the mythologizing leanings of Christian Rosencreutz, who wants to ensure male power ascendancy by sacrificing Fevvers, which endanger her. His is a Gothic palace, his world one of masculine power, *The Times*, leather seats, and a 'phallus rampant' as emblem. Significantly, Rosencreutz spouts his own heresies about gender differences, but their resemblance to real literary, medical, philosophical and political arguments against women's emancipation in the nineteenth century make him culturally representative of historical oppression and destruction. He argues that:

> women are of a different soul-substance from men, cut from a different bolt of spirit cloth, and altogether too pure and rarefied to be bothering their pretty little heads with things of this world, such as the Irish question, and the Boer war.

(p.78)

Rosencreutz casts Fevvers as a sacrificial figure, but she escapes. Later, the Grand Duke wants to turn Fevvers into a golden bird in a golden cage (like Yeats's golden bird on a golden bough, in 'Sailing to Byzantium'). Woman is an art object for the Duke, and his collection, including woman as Aeolian (wind) harp, will be crowned by the ultimate exchange for jewels, Fevvers reduced to a tiny priceless golden bird filling the empty perch in the empty cage among the Fabergé egg constructions. The ice swan downstairs, reminiscent of Leda and the Swan, twin to the swan on top of the cage, melts as Fevvers's time drips out, but she manipulates the Duke's own sexual needs to engineer her escape. While she 'contemplated life as a toy' (p.192), she ensures the Duke's climax coincides with the wet crash of the ice sculpture, and her own exit, leaping onto a model train which, fantasy intermingled with realism, turns into the full-size 'real' trans-Siberian railway. Fevvers's sexual energy triumphs. She defines and retains her own identity, revealing it to none, fooling Walser the journalist whose quest for the 'real' matches our own, and taking control of her own myth. She celebrates her life and her own sexuality, as the novel forces readers to redefine the boundaries of the real and the fantastic. Artifice, literary and artistic representations and mythic constructions are all deconstructed and reconstructed.

USE OF THE GOTHIC AS A SOCIAL CRITIQUE

Nights at the Circus examines myths and constructions of femininity through the arch construction herself, Fevvers. Angela Carter's Gothic, highly intertextual brand of magic realism ideally provides both an ironic critique of the power upheld through myths and symbols, creating and re-creating new myths and symbols enabling a theft of power, a flight from patriarchy. Woman as bird does not have to be caged, and flight suggests power and freedom, not a desperate escape.

In fiction, magic realism is best suited to express that mixture of the factual, social, historical world, and the imaginative, fantastic, spiritual magical other world, largely denied in our scientific, 'rational' times. With the reinvestment of the magical and the imaginative comes an investigation into those limiting social practices which have led to the repression of the different, of woman, of black and minority cultures. Some writers like Angela Carter and Fay Weldon start with traditional and contemporary mythic representations and take them to logical extremes, enabling the powers of the magical and the spiritual to have equal value with the everyday.

HORROR

Horror is a more violent, terrifying branch of the Gothic. In conventional horror, women are figured as monsters or, as automata, dolls, as explored and critiqued in 'The Loves of Lady Purple' and *The Magic Toyshop*. In these roles, women end up disempowered, destroyed and punished. Icons of femininity, the focus of a destructive adulation, they are sacrificed or rescued by heroes into domestic bliss. The roles men play in such conventional forms are also stereotypical: patriarchal bullies, whether fathers or Grand Dukes.

Conventional horror disturbs the familiar and dramatizes what we fear most – usually deceptive, destructive potential or the absence of what we take for granted, our identity, families, relationships, the real, homely, safe, the everyday. It expresses as 'other' terrifying, not familiar, not us, that which we fear. In so doing, it sets up various polarities.

Instead of the familiar and attractive we have the unfamiliar, strange, unattractive, the monstrous. But the genre is also conventional in that, once it has exposed and dramatized our worst fears, it returns us to safety and order, reinforcing the status quo. We are left feeling safe with the homely, but only if we can spot what is threatening because it is different, or other. As such, then, the genre can also reinforce a kind of social xenophobia: anyone or anything out of the ordinary is suspect. But horror in the hands of more radical writers, such as Angela Carter, can question such simplistic responses, such essentially conservative, indeed blinkered, possibly tyrannical, repressive world views. In Carter's hands, horror refuses to restore a limiting status quo.

Central to Carter's rewriting of conventional horror is the breaking down of established philosophical and cultural binary oppositions, that is, male/female, good/bad, day/night, normal/other. Her horror fiction casts a critical eye on society and its myths which consistently configure women as the desired or feared other. She defamiliarizes the (precariously) comfortable everyday world which is premised upon controlling women's sexuality, forms of social deviance and other threats to social order, defined as familiar manifestations of patriarchy: the domestic world, home ownership, white-male controlled economic and sexual power and so on. In challenging the oppressive norms of patriarchy, Carter challenges what is considered the basis for horror, that is, whatever transgresses these norms, subverts these beliefs, threatens this security. She overturns what is normally considered terrifying, writes from a perspective more likely to be that of women (and other marginalized groups) and exposes and subverts what, for horror, is a new target, the seamy and sadistic side of patriarchal controls. In so doing, she actually reclaims the subversive powers of horror, using it as form and forum to act out disturbing critical fantasies, to articulate what Western culture tends to ignore and refuse. In her hands, the seemingly adored but ultimately locked up, disempowered and sexually victimized 'living doll' escapes the domestic trap, celebrating her own identity and sexual power.

Angela Carter has several favourites in her horror writing. One is woman as doll, puppet or object. Celluloid constructions are figures frequently marking the threshold of horror and comedy in Carter. Uncle Philip aims to turn his hapless extended family into puppets, and to control Melanie's sexuality.

Angela Carter also explores the underlying tensions of popular tales. Lizzie Borden ('The Fall River Axe Murders') who 'took an axe and gave her father forty whacks' murders her family, but we never know why. Carter suggests Lizzie is the product of the hothouse pressure of turn-of-the-century USA where girls were briefly allowed out on European tours and into high society. They marry, or not, and that is the end: their fates are sealed. After a brief but limited set of opportunities they are either incarcerated in their own family home as mother, or back in the paternal home.

Lizzie Borden lives in an undertaker's. She is a social victim and her life is all dead ends. Issues of space and confinement inform our reading of Lizzie's constraints living in a domestic labyrinth representing her own repression in:

> a house full of locked doors that open only into other rooms with other locked doors, for, upstairs and downstairs, all the rooms lead in and out of another like a maze in a bad dream.

> (p.304)

There is bound to be an explosion, culturally produced. On a sour morning of intense heat, she discovers her hated stepmother has butchered her favourite pigeons for a pie. Lizzie's response is to retaliate in kind. Carter does not bother to depict the carnage; she leaves us poised on the threshold of the tragedy, horrified. Lizzie's explosion rocks family structures.

CARNIVAL AND REVERSALS – CELEBRATING DIFFERENCE AND USING COMEDY

In conventional horror women represent a threat to male security of identity, a sense of stability in the 'real' shared world. Carter's women put this loss of identity to their political advantage. *Nights at the Circus* (1984) is more akin to carnival than horror, but its larger than life carnivalesque heroine, Fevvers, negotiates a virtual obstacle course of potentially disempowering, reifying situations which could easily turn to the stuff of horror were she not to use her imagination, self-awareness and her physical presence as a woman to escape and have the last laugh. Christian Rosencreutz, Carter's anti-feminist activist in *Nights at the Circus* feels a threat to his sense of personal, gendered security at the spectacle of the rampant aerialiste Fevvers. Rosencreutz's esoteric chanting is a patriarchally constructed and maintained linguistic myth and mastery undercut by Fevvers's mix of the Cockney commonsensical and the erudite. To Rosencreutz, Fevvers is an icon of terrifying desire, and threat, Venus and Achmatoth, love and death:

> Lady of the hub of the celestial wheel, creature half of earth and half of air, virgin and whore, reconciler of fundament and firmament, reconciler or opposing states through the mediation of your ambivalent body.

> (p.59)

Fevvers chooses flight, escaping from his plan to deify then destroy her. Carter's slapstick and irony fuel the dramatization of this confrontation of the historically and mythically aware, spirited, carnivalesque woman's voice against the fear and loathing of this oppressive male. Carter's jaunty debunking of male-defined horror, the sexualized, powerful woman, represents a political harnessing of energy.

Michel Foucault a theoretician of sexuality and power (*A History of Sexuality*, 1976) relates power, law, language and sex/desire/identity. At different moments in history, he argues, power structures dictate and construct the versions of and validations of sexuality, sexual relationships, desire and sexual identity, and do so through language, including images and myths. If and when we can realize that such representations and constraints are socially and historically constructed, perpetuated by language and myth, we can imagine things could be otherwise. Taking a feminist angle, Kristeva in *Powers of Horror* (1984) explores how and why conventional male representations of women figure them as, on the one hand, sexually dangerous, to be constrained, owned, their individuality a challenge and, on the other, unblemished, pure, vulnerable, delicate pieces of property, sexually ignorant, passive, vulnerable, potentially innocent victims. These linked representations spring from male fears of women's individualism and sexuality. They result in refusal of knowledge and power, and in myths and popular cultural norms advising, establishing models for girls to dedicate their lives to serving others as humble, simple, silenced wives. They also result in the flip side of what could be seen as protective, caring behaviour – brutality and constraint, denial of freedom, destruction and silencing. In *The Magic Toyshop*, the tale of orphaned Melanie provides a critique of such sexual power games. In so doing, it exposes ways in which a variety of myths and texts operate to condition the expectations and constraints on girls and women. But Melanie eventually manages to escape and the novel ends with her and Irish Finn poised on the edge of a potential new life.

Romantic fictions are undercut, and various myths and formulae overturned. Carter's carnivalesque, celebratory work rewrites myths and roles for women and men, using the Gothic and horror as well as romantic fictional formulae and (in *The Passion of New Eve*) science fictional elements. While Carter attacks myths produced under patriarchy, she is no blinkered feminist, she also sends up goddess myths as constraining. Carter exposes the lies and constraints by which we are constructed and governed, the myths and the reportage which misrepresent and limit us. In *Nights at the Circus* winged woman, the aerialiste Fevvers, a Cockney showgirl at the turn of the century is the embodiment of woman as 'bird'. She spends much of her young adult life resisting the mythologizing constraints which various tyrannical and threatened men try to impose upon her. Anti-suffrage (women's right to vote) politician, Christian Rosencreutz, mythologizes her as Sophia, semi-angel who must be destroyed (he thinks) for masculine power and the world to continue. A Grand Duke tries to reduce her to the size and status of a toy. Carter uses magic realism, horror and humour to critique ways in which power dictates its law to sex and constrains people's (mainly women's) freedom to develop their own sexuality and identities.

Angela Carter's fiction casts a critical eye on society and its myths of economic and sexual power, and the constructions of gendered identities. In challenging the oppressive norms of patriarchy, Carter critiques the powers of cultural myths, popular fictions and horror, reinstating them as forms and forums for exploring and embodying alternative versions of gendered relations, sexual energies and individual self-awareness. She does this by combining opposites in her work using images of twinning and mirrors, and the form of the oxymoron, and she scrutinizes forms of horror, Gothic, the fantastic, subverting them, showing their sources, replacing them finally with something alternative and celebratory, with the carnivalesque and the comic, the amusing and the everyday.

✳ ✳ ✳ SUMMARY ✳ ✳ ✳

We have looked at Carter's themes in terms of:

● critiquing constructions and representations of gender and power.

● demythologizing cultural myths found in fairy tales, high art, popular culture and film, rewriting horror and the Gothic to do so.

● exploring sexual energies, both the rather seamy, oppressive and the liberating.

● celebrating the energies of individuals, often those who have been 'otherized', silenced and misunderstood because of gender, race or social position, using images of the carnival and reversals of power.

Major Works

5

'To think I really fooled you!' she marvelled. 'It just goes to show there's nothing like confidence.'

(Angela Carter, *Nights at the Circus*, p.295)

Angela Carter is mainly known for her novels and short stories of which *The Magic Toyshop*, *Nights at the Circus* and the collection *Burning your Boats* are probably the most popular. She produced several novels from *Shadow Dance* in 1966, a dramatically rather static, vicious representation of the superficiality of sexual power games and sometimes pointless, vacuous, threatening lifestyle of a group of Bohemian youth in 1960s Bristol, to, in 1991, the year before she died, *Wise Children*, a lavish, sometimes dark, sprawling comedy. This last work, set from the 1940s through to (nearly) the end of the twentieth century, resembles Shakespeare's comedies in its critical vigour and celebration of human energies. Carter's critical, celebratory, overwritten, humorous and rather subversive work also encompasses a number of short stories, some of which are retold fairy tales, and several lively, culturally focused essays, plays and poetry.

THE MAGIC TOYSHOP (1967)

The Magic Toyshop focuses on the adolescence of a young girl, Melanie, who, orphaned goes to live with her abusive toyshop-owning Uncle Philip, her silenced, caring Irish Aunt Margaret, and Aunt Margaret's brothers, Francie and Finn. It is a rites-of-passage novel, following part of a year in the adolescent life of Melanie, 15 when the story opens. *The Magic Toyshop* mixes humour and terror in exposing potential gendered and cultural oppressions in both the family and twentieth-century British society. Through exploring the life of orphaned Melanie and her siblings in the house of arch (really quite Victorian and Dickensian, that is, bullying, old-fashioned and repressive) patriarch Uncle Philip, *The Magic Toyshop* portrays and critiques representations and constructions of gender and power. In many ways a *Bildungsroman* or story of a young person growing up and developing, the novel puts England under the spotlight with its antiquated imperialist heritage, its dingy lower middle-class housing, its dominant father figures and small-minded class, gender and culture-ridden prejudices.

Melanie and Finn survey the burning toyshop

Influences: reading and the cinema

Carter was extremely well and widely read and also an avid cinemagoer. Her works and intertextual references suggest we conjure up and interpret our worlds through reading and other social influences. *The Magic Toyshop* is replete with references to high art and fiction including Dickens, whose rather grim and gritty, often exaggerated and symbolic descriptions, emerge in the constrained, manipulated world of the London toyshop in which Melanie and her brother and sister go to live.

Another key reference in the novel is the Leda and the Swan myth, favourite Carter shorthand (it appears again in *Nights at the Circus* and several short stories) for all those cultural myths which depict women as puppets and victims under patriarchal power.

Women and representations

Melanie is an individual but also, as an adolescent girl, represents many women trying to find out what their identities are within the limited opportunities available. She finds the representations of women with which she can identify are all produced by male artists, scientists and writers, even down to popular fictions for girls and Hollywood movies about romance and marriage. Initially she 'tries on' versions of what it might mean to be a grown up, middle-class woman like her mother, putting on her mother's wedding dress, imagining herself an adult and finding both that her body shape (she is too small, undeveloped) denies this version of herself and her youthful energies refuse to so constrain her. In a symbolic moment Melanie, in the cold, enormous wedding dress, gets locked outside her house in the night-time garden and in climbing back in through the window to get back to bed and safety, ruins the dress. It is suggested that she is not ready for such a version of womanhood. However, on the death of her parents in an aircrash while on a lecture tour, she and her brother and sister, orphaned, have to move in with Uncle Philip. Here Melanie is forced to act out the mythical part of Leda in toyshop-owner Uncle Philip's puppet theatre play of Leda and the Swan, and so to play a part of a woman dominated by men, gods and creatures.

The Victorian, domineering uncle is criticized throughout the text. This both exposes the kind of bullying male power which is allowed free rein in many families, and the *imperial* bullying of national powers. Margaret, Francie and Finn are all Irish, and historically the Irish have been seen as 'ungovernable subjects', to be restrained. But the Irish have also always been represented as subversive and imaginative, linked to the world of the supernatural.

Melanie and romance

Melanie's romance ideal is later shattered in her relationship with the coarse but friendly Finn, whose rough dirtiness initially horrifies her. Finn's version of a midnight garden contains a fallen idol of Queen Victoria, face down in the mud and vandalized with sexual graffiti. Melanie, disillusioned, identifies with the statue which itself represents disillusionment, the end of the British Empire, its controls over other peoples and its grandeur. This, and her realization that Finn is sent by her Uncle Philip, the puppet master, to rape her, leads to her own demythologizing, or her rejection of the various initially attractive but ultimately constraining myths and dreams about romance and her life as a woman. Melanie realizes that in the end, Finn (rather than a smooth Hollywood romantic fiction hero) is likely to be her mate. She compares ideal and real.

The Leda and the Swan episode

The most powerful moment in the novel is the enactment of the Leda and the Swan rape scene with Melanie forced to be a human puppet to Uncle Philip's fantasy of power. In high art there are several representations of the story of Leda and the Swan, always with an adoring Leda cuddling a beautiful, powerful yet kindly swan. But the actual myth is rather unappealing. Jove, king of the gods, descends to a variety of 'lucky' women, each time in the shape of a beast, as a bull to Europa, a swan to Leda, and a shower of gold to Danae. The resultant rape is always depicted in positive tones in art, and the myth suggests that woman is lucky to carry the seed of the gods, even if the power of an animal is mixed into the act. W.B. Yeats's poem 'Leda and the Swan' hauntingly and langorously portrays the strangeness and the frightening (because of the non-human bird) yet rapturous (because of the god, and the sexual power) lack of resistance by Leda to the rape: 'those terrified vague fingers' are Leda's 'so caught up'. The poem emphasizes the strangeness and the power, but wallows in the sexual frissons at the same time. Carter uses 'loins' and some other of the same words as Yeats to indicate the poem as source, but she simultaneously actualizes the horror and brutality of the act, and the ridiculousness of Western male-dominated civilization's imagining and repeatedly redescribing this myth of power and subordination. Melanie 'felt herself not herself' she has her identity wrested from her with the descent of the puppet swan; feathers fill her mouth; she screams: 'the obscene swan had mounted her' and the near rape of girl by man-controlled, man-constructed beast of power is plain, violent, real and monstrous. But while the full reality of the horror of this enacted

KEY FACT

Leda and the Swan is an ancient myth which celebrates the rape of Leda by Zeus, king of the Gods, carrying out his intention to couple with mortal women and produce children both human and godlike. It is the subject of Renaissance paintings and of Yeats's poem.

power relationship is emphasized, it is also debunked, satirized, laughed at. 'Like fate or the clock', the plywood puppet is operated by a bully who pictures himself as godlike, caught up in his own myth of power, on his own petty stage in the toyshop which is his world. Philip thinks of himself as having a sonorous voice, wreaking the will of 'Almighty Jove' but he is simultaneously a figure of fun, and a microcosmic figure of patriarchal power. The swan is a slapstick production: 'On came the swan, its feet going splat, splat, splat' (p.166). Carter enables us to laugh, to see the whole pretence as ridiculous, but also to feel that its reality is tangibly oppressive, real and fantastic at once. Laughter and deconstruction give the readers more power than Finn, who smashes the swan but can be smashed himself.

Why select this myth and weave it into a tale about a young British girl? Carter points out that literature and myth consistently configure women as dangerous and to blame because of their beauty. By replaying the myth in a toyshop basement, Carter shows up both the absurdity and potential danger of adopting values based on such myths. Melanie loses her sense of identity in the ritual. Uncle Philip's power could turn Melanie into a victim, but the comedy of the narrative style undercuts and lets us critique this.

The energies of the comic give characters and readers some way of fighting back, seeing what dominates as ridiculous, hinting at new ways of being.

BURNING YOUR BOATS: COLLECTED STORIES (1996)

Burning your Boats collects together all Carter's published short stories including the early *Fireworks* and *The Bloody Chamber* along with the later tales. Angela Carter's stories, such as 'The Company of Wolves' often utilize folk myth and fairy tale, in this case the 'Little Red Riding Hood' story, to expose ways in which conventional myths, parables and fairy tales control our perceptions by portraying relationships of gender and power. They are also entertaining rewrites which overturn conventional values and endings, challenging behavioural norms (which the tales reinforce). In Carter's rewritten version of fairy tales, myths and legends such as 'Beauty and the Beast,' ('The Courtship of Mr Lyon'; 'The Tiger's Bride'), and 'Bluebeard' ('The Bloody Chamber') women generally have the upper hand, reversing the sexist bias of conventional fairy tales.

'The Company of Wolves' follows the traditional Red Riding Hood tale in so far as Rosaleen is warned not to wander in the woods when she takes the basket of goodies to Granny, Granny is devoured by the wolf, and the wolf and Rosaleen establish a threatening question and answer exchange. But, arriving at Granny's house, Rosaleen, far from falling victim to the male sadist, the wolf, subdues him, turning into a werewolf herself, throwing her clothes into the fire with his. 'If there's a beast in men it meets its match in women too' notes Rosaleen's mother.

Vampires and puppets

In 'The Loves of Lady Purple' and 'Lady in the House of Love', Carter uses vampire myths to explore ways in which women are made victims to structures and beliefs embedded in romantic fictions. 'The Loves of Lady Purple' follows the revenge of a puppet operated by an inscrutable Eastern professor who nightly forces her to enact sado-masochistic scenarios. One night when he hangs her up and kisses her, she takes her

Lady Purple takes her revenge

revenge, comes alive and drains him of his blood, walking off into the village nearby to establish herself in a brothel. He is destroyed, but her successful escape is interestingly curtailed by the inability to imagine another life than one dependent on sex for money, not unlike the dreams enacted for the professor and her nightly audiences.

In 'Lady in the House of Love', a glamorous, reluctant vampire, relative of Vlad the Impaler (the model for Dracula), feeds nightly on small animals due to both her own squeamishness and the limited supply of human blood. When a visiting First World War soldier drops in, she falls in love. He has no idea that in kissing the blood on her hand he awakens mortal desire in her, which kills her. The tale undermines the lies of romantic fictions which promise eternity to lovers, but it also turns the tables on vampire fictions which would have predatory vampires victimizing the innocent. This innocent young man cannot make connections with the rose he removes from the lady of the house, and her demise. She literally dies for love.

Lizzie Borden took an axe and gave her father forty whacks

Other tales explore relationships of gender and power and use the characteristics of horror in doing so. 'The Fall Rivers Axe Murders' shows the horrific repercussions of late nineteenth/early twentieth-century American middle-class constraints on women when Lizzie Borden, oppressed in her society and home, 'took an axe and gave her father forty whacks'.

THE PASSION OF NEW EVE (1977)
Situated in a grim futuristic version of 1960s USA, with African Americans taking over New York in tanks, burning Grand Central Station, while women take to the streets engaging in guerrilla warfare with men, Carter's feminist science fiction tale conjures a post-apocalyptic world dominated by gender and power struggles. Characters and issues are a direct product of Carter's fascination with Hollywood. *The Passion of New Eve* reveals how popular culture perpetuates stereotypical, artificial representations of women and men.

The novel is concerned with a science fictional experiment taking sexist Evelyn and turning him into his own (abused) version of a woman, a bimbo, letting him loose to suffer in a world which silences and disempowers women. Evelyn sexually uses, then deserts Leilah, but he becomes fixated with her sexually, seeking the 'exquisite negative of her sex' (p.27). Captured by female guerrillas, he is taken to Beulah, an underground city where he is raped, castrated and then becomes a guinea pig for a sex change on the orders of the ruler, Mother, a bizarre parody of women and goddess myths. Mother, bearded, resembles Queen Hatshepsut and, like a sow, has several rows of nipples. Her intent is to overwhelm and castrate the universe run by men: 'I am the Great Paricide, I am the Castratrix of the Phallocentric universe, I am Mama, Mama, Mama!' (p.67). It is important to recognize that Carter is equally parodying and critiquing mythical, matriarchal and patriarchal excesses.

Eve (now called) has as a man, spent hours in the cinema and fallen in love with screen goddess (and transvestite) Tristessa, whose repeated movie role is one of beautiful woman whose attractiveness is heightened by sadness. Viewers/voyeurs revel in the artifice, and in the conjunction of sex and sadness, sex and death. But, as a transvestite (Tristessa does not go as far as the operation to become a transsexual) her home is totally artificial, as artificial, it is suggested as the gender roles in which people are imprisoned. The house and pool are sterile, static, brittle and easily destroyed. Eve, kidnapped by the tyrannical sexist Zero, (based on Charles Manson, notorious California cult leader who butchered actress Sharon Tate and her friends in the 1960s) is forced into a raiding party which destroys Tristessa's home. The women of Zero's harem are abused, Tristessa tormented. This unpleasant, oppressive world is a future projection of the faults of our own: gender stereotyping and tyranny, debilitating myths, artifice replacing life. The tale critiques popular cultural representations of gender but also mid-1960s/1970s myths of nurturing all-women communities, so showing Carter to be far from a stereotypical feminist writer. *The Passion of New Eve* is an apocalyptic Gothic, science fiction work.

NIGHTS AT THE CIRCUS (1984)

'Lor' love you, sir!' Fevvers sang out in a voice that clanged like dustbin lids. 'As to my place of birth, why, I first saw light of day right here in smoky old London, didn't I! Not billed the "Cockney Venus", for nothing, sir, though they could just as well 'ave called me "Helen of the High Wire", due to the unusual circumstances in which I come ashore – for I never docked via what you might call the *normal channels*, sir, oh, dear me, no; but, just like Helen of Troy, was *hatched*.

(p.7)

Probably Carter's greatest work, *Nights at the Circus* is rich with intertextual references to poetry and novels, to Yeats, Dickens, Zola and Shakespeare among others. Perched on the cusp between the nineteenth and twentieth centuries, it provides a historically rich, fantastically laden exploration of ways in which women are mythologized, constructed as saints or whores. It suggests new potential for woman in the volatile period of 'the New Woman' at the nineteenth century's end, leading to suffragettes and social changes in the next century.

Fevvers, winged woman and high wire performer, is the novel's central figure and we follow her various exploits and adventures as she moves from Paris to Russia to England, protecting herself from predatory men, seeking ways to be successful while developing and retaining her sense of identity. Throughout, the novel questions reality and fantasy, critiquing oppressive gender stereotypes and relationships of power.

The clock stands fixed at midnight in both the brothel and the dressing room as Fevvers and Lizzie tell their story to the brash, young, fact-finding American reporter, Walser, who wishes to expose Fevvers in a few well-chosen words, but who ends up as circus clown, chicken, novice shaman and, finally, Fevvers's lover, dancing to her tune. It is in 'the hour of vision and revelation, the still hour in the centre of the storm of time' (p.29) a very modernist moment, when the magical details of the story pour out, claimed as truth. Fevvers and her story

Fevvers, the cockney Venus aerialiste

provide a parallel to Carter's fantastic, Gothic, engaged art. Elaborate fantasy and material historical engagement are not mutually exclusive: the one is vehicle for the other in Carter's work. And readers are rather like Walser, fascinated, seeking truth but mesmerized by fantasy and storytelling.

Art and life

Nights at the Circus is concerned with the power of the imagination, art's ability to represent and manage, avoiding reduction and rigidity. Like Fevvers, the work calls attention to itself: polemic is translated into a rococo style replete with literary and cultural echoes. And like Fevvers, perhaps, 'In a secular age, an authentic miracle must purport to be a hoax, in order to gain credit in the world' (p.17). It has a compelling control of narrative and reader.

'To think I really fooled you!' she marvelled. 'It just goes to show there's nothing like confidence.

(p.295)

The mocking remarks with which Fevvers embraces Walser at the novel's end echo how we as readers feel about it – it questions our versions of what is real, what constructed, what fantasy, and how we might highlight oppressive constructions as fantasies, while using our imaginations to suggest life could be otherwise.

Fevvers is larger than life, part of the popular imagination, both earthy (her voice like dustbin lids) and fantastic – she has wings. Like the book, she mixes the everyday and the magical.

Questioning and challenging gender stereotypes

Nights at the Circus examines constructions of femininity through Fevvers. Energetic, combining interest in love and material things with self-preservation, Fevvers has many close escapes from victimization by various domineering, vicious, autocratic men including a Grand Duke and a Rosicrucian politician.

Fevvers is a construct, an icon, imagined version of woman, figurehead and muse. Like Melanie in *The Magic Toyshop*, she is no fool for myth and romance, controlling her own identity. Fevvers is both angel and whore, the logical embodiment of patriarchy's dichotomous construction of woman. Contraries combine in her, fantasy made real, a material product of late Victorianism. As an adolescent, Carter has her posing in Ma Nelson's brothel, as 'winged Venus', with a short sword as protective emblem. Later, in the Circus, decked out in the trappings of elaborate falseness, dyed feathers and a trapeze hinting that her flight is but an act, she tantalizes the imagination and the reason alike. Vulnerable because of her sex and wings, Fevvers would be just a freak were her true nature exposed, but artifice and mystery protect her. Those who seek to master and expose her represent both man's power over woman and the destructive power of reductionism.

Fevvers's common sense protects her from harm when those of perversity and power try to dominate and destroy their ideal construction of the feminine. Early on she realizes:

> Sealed in this artificial egg, this sarcophagus of beauty, I waited, I waited … although I could not have told you for what it was I waited. Except, I assure you, I did *not* await the kiss of a magic prince, sir! With my two eyes I nightly saw how such a kiss would seal me up in my *appearance* for ever!
>
> (p. 39)

The cold light of day reveals the decay and artifice surrounding the whores when Ma Nelson dies. In a glass the woman see 'the hags we would become and knew that we too, like pleasures, were mortal' (p.49), whereupon all solidity seems to dissolve. Fevvers is herself reified, a victim of necessity under capitalist and patriarchal society, forced to pose among other 'women monsters' for the titillation of the perverse customers of the notorious Madame Schreck in a money-oriented sado-masochistic influenced Gothic brothel. Like a black widow spider, Madam Schreck is a miser whose house resembles a living death, a gallery of *tableaux vivants* in 'profane altars' (p.61), of which de Sade would be proud.

Fevvers keeps her eye out for cash and escape, but her own capitalist tendencies nearly cause her downfall. Her first adventure is on her night out with Christian Rosencreutz, the embodiment of patriarchal oppression, capitalism and perversion, a combination nearly lethal for the 'only fully feathered intacta in the entire history of the world' (p.71). The Gothic Rosencreutz's reading of mythology labels Fevvers as Flora, and he casts her as sacrificial victim to provide his route to eternal life.

The central episode, Fevvers's second lucky escape from being turned into a concrete myth, takes place at the Grand Duke's house and focuses attention on both the construction of femininity and the relation of this construction, this oppressive reification, to a rigidly sterile, materialistic worldview fostered by patriarchy under capitalism. The house Fevvers approaches is filled with priceless, static objects of ornament:

> His house was the realm of minerals, of metals of vitrification – of gold, marble and crystal; pale halls and endless mirrors and glittering chandeliers that clanged like wind-bells in the draught from the front door ... and a sense of frigidity, of sterility almost palpable, almost tangible in the hard, chill surfaces and empty spaces.

> Always the same! thought Fevvers censoriously. Money is wasted on the rich.

(p.184)

The Grand Duke prefers automata, and owns a miniature orchestra constructed of semi-precious stones and birds' plumage, for which he murdered a mandarin. They 'had the authentically priceless glamour of objects intended only for pleasure, the impure alloy of the absolutely functionless' (p.188). Woman is the chief subject of the Duke's penchant for artifice. A hollow harp woman makes music which is 'mathematical', frozen, otherworldly. Everywhere Fevvers sees versions of herself. An ice sculpture of her which wears a priceless necklace is the key figure. The Duke promises that she too will melt as the sculpture does, and she doubts this, mistaking his predatory remark for sexual advance when he really intends a more final mastery. There is also a miniature of her in one of his jeweller's shop, Fabergé eggs. As the ice drips, and she plays his sexual game in order to secure the promised gifts, so Fevvers is led further into danger. Just prior to the Duke's climax she realizes that there is a golden cage open and ready for her:

> It was white gold and topped with a lovely swan, a tribute, perhaps, to her putative paternity. And, as she suspected, it contained a cage made out of gold wires with, inside, a little perch of rubies and of sapphires and of diamonds, the good old red, white and blue.

(p.192)

She recognizes what he has in mind for her – to own her and turn her into an ornament: 'The cage was empty. No bird stood on that perch, yet Fevvers did not shrink, but was at once aware of the hideous possibility she might do so' (p.192). The ice carving collapses, and she escapes from life as a bird in a golden cage, ruffled, torn, without her new jewels, grateful to just catch the train to Russia with the Circus.

The circus: an imaginative alternative?

The novel interrogates social and cultural constructions of femininity. But it goes much further, exposing the false dichotomy between reason and the imagination. The circus embodies illusion and variety, an alternative to the hard facts, as it does, for example in Dickens's *Hard Times*. In the circus, Fevvers can perform, testing the credulity of those around her. Art and life, she is a living embodiment of a fantasy emphasizing the performativity of gender, identity and the difficulty of telling the difference between what might be artifice and what might be real when everything is a construction and a performance, a version.

A crucial moment is when the circus aerialiste shows (probably) that she really can fly, 'Fevvers, remember, was six feet two in her stockinged feet and turned the scale at fourteen English stone' (p.159).

> Yet those marmoreal, immense arms and legs of hers, as they made leisurely, swimming movements through the air, looked palely unconvincing, as if arbitrarily tacked on to the bird attire…whilst convincing others, she herself remained unconvinced about the precise nature of her own illusion.
>
> (pp.159–60)

The Charivaris, fellow performers jealous of the public's interest in Fevver's act, have rigged the machinery, and a rope snaps. Their intention must be to maim her or prove her false. Fevvers calls their bluff. She does not plummet to her death when the cut rope snaps – she flies and 'She even poked out her tongue' (p.159).

The circus is a mixture of everyday reality and the fantastic, a microcosm and construction which enables us to cast a critical eye on the relationships and realities of our own world. It contains hierarchies, wife-beating strong men, sharp practice, brutality and power based on capitalism, but offers opportunities for reform. The strong man learns to be meek and kindly, the caged beasts escape into fantasy worlds as tigers reflected in mirror shards. The performers, the princess and Mignon, settle comfortably in a house of women.

The animals in Colonel Kierney's circus desert, die or dissolve, as do the musically controlled tigers, whose source lies in William Blake's 'Tyger', rather than the circus animals of W.B. Yeats, and who embody beauty, power, and the resources of imagination. Their status is rendered increasingly imaginative when the tigers reappear on the roof while the princess plays the piano in a house in the wilderness. The clowns desert and, finally, so does the Colonel with his oracular pig, Sybil, leaving behind Fevvers, winged miracle. *Nights at the Circus* resembles Yeats's last poems in its debate about the source of symbolism in the everyday, earthiness and the necessity for interrelation between the contraries of reason and imagination. These references to Yeats, combined with other modernist asides, run throughout the novel.

Walser the new man

Much of Carter's work scrutinizes ways in which masculinity is represented, critiquing constructions of power. Walser, the journalist, is like the reader, seeking something real. He initially desires to expose her pretence but then recognizes the importance of Fevver's ownership of her own version of her identity. 'She owes it to herself to remain a woman, he thought. It is her human duty. As a symbolic woman, she has a meaning, as an anomaly, none' (p.161). Later, Walser himself becomes a new man. He casts off the trappings of the nineteenth-century Victorian world and its obsessions with defining and fixing reality, lives with a shaman and turns himself into a human chicken, re-emerging enlightened, if a little dazed.

Walser newly fledged from his experience with a shaman

The new century and new possibilities

At the turning point of the century, in the novel, apocalyptic imagery of whirlwinds and frightening changes suggest the questioning of fixed beliefs. Two versions of the new century and New Woman appear. Sleeping Beauty at Madame Schreck's sinks further into paralysing dreams of the coming century. Fevvers, winged wonder, embodies the New Woman's flight from the bondage of her roles: 'And once the old world has turned on its axle so that the new dawn can dawn, then, ah, then! all the women will have wings, the same as I' (p.285). But Carter leaves open both her fate and that of the new century.

Nights at the Circus is difficult to sum up because it is so rich, open-ended and multilayered. The story might finish as the new century dawns but the issues with which it deals do not suddenly turn two-dimensional and dissolve as artifice, as do the tigers turning into mirrors after the train crash wrecks the circus. The novel raises issues relating equally to philosophy as to gender and power. Energies and laughter end the book, myths and century:

> The spiralling tornado of Fevver's laughter began to twist and shudder across the entire globe, as if a spontaneous response to the giant comedy that endlessly unfolded beneath it, until everything that lived and breathed, everywhere was laughing.

> (p.295)

WISE CHILDREN (1991)

> Sometimes I think, if I look hard enough, I can see back into the past. There goes the wind, again. Crash. Over goes the dustbin, all the trash spills out … empty cat-food cans, cornflakes packets, laddered tights, tea leaves.

> (p.3)

Wise Children, Carter's last novel, is in the fashion of Shakesperean comedies: sprawling, filled with characters and whimsy, action and humour, escapes and fantasies, celebratory. The novel focuses on the adventures of Nora and Dora Chance, ageing illegitimate twins of a great Shakespearean actor Sir Melchior Hazard. Minor actresses and music hall 'hoofers', they take part in the 1940s Hollywood version of *A Midsummer Night's Dream*, their adventures and those of the production team and large cast as magical, funny, celebratory, dependent upon cross-dressing and as critical as the Shakespeare play itself. Dramatic, *Wise Children* is filled with lively, occasionally coarse references such as: 'We used to be song and dance girls. We can still lift a leg higher than your average dog, if called for' (pp.1–2).

A warm, lively and critical comic novel

While the novel concentrates on Carter's favourite themes of identity, gender roles, construction, representations and performance, it is also comic, lively and warm, celebrating maturity, the energies and imaginative wisdom of old age.

Nora and Dora Chance dance on into the new century

The novel has an immediacy and a lively tone, produced by its first-person narrator, Dora Chance, who points out that as a woman from a working-class background, she will present us with unconventional, alternative versions of events and values. She also represents alternative versions of Bristol, London, the South and the lower middle class. The opening is immediate and personal, set in a real place and time.

Carter's mixture of magic and realism predominates, and her sense of the everyday is tangibly created in vignettes of South London and class difference over time. While she rarely concentrates on realistic detail as a historical record, Carter here re-creates a changing London most credibly in a way a realist writer would be proud of:

> Once upon a time, you could make a crude distinction, thus: the rich
> lived amidst pleasant verdure in the North speedily whisked to exclusive
> shopping by abundant public transport while the poor eked out
> miserable existences in the South in circumstances of urban deprivation

condemned to wait for hours at windswept bus-stops while sounds of marital violence, breaking glass and drunken song echoed around and it was cold and dark and smelled of fish and chips.

(p.1)

Always concentrating on change, Carter here points out through Dora Chance that South London is rising socially. The language is authentic London, cliché ridden, racy, mixed with something more journalistic:

You'd never believe the price of a house round here, these days. And what does the robin do then, poor thing?

Bugger the robin!   (p.12)

Dora, Nora (and Carter) use everyday speech, idiom and cliché to evoke everyday lives. Their lives are seedy but celebrate the energy, artifice and imagination of performance. Bacon, face cream and marmalade all evoke their dated but lively existence. Their home is chaotic:

Hello, hello … here comes one of the pussy cats, out of the wardrobe, stretching and yawning. She can smell the bacon. There's another, white, with marmalade patches, sleeping on my pillow. Dozens more roam freely. The house smells of cat, a bit, but more of geriatric chlorine – cold cream, face powder, dress preservers, old fags, stale tea.

(pp.1–2)

Part of the reason for Dora's memoirs is her desire to fix and label the past. This she does with energy using first photo albums as jumping-off points to re-create the past lives of the twins both for themselves and for listeners, us. Absent fathers and maternal grandmothers litter their lives and 'Entertainment' runs in the family. Their niece Tiffany hosts on the television. As performers, their work spans the best part of the century. Dora, Nora, doubles, cast a critical and amused eye on the world they entertain and act out. Their position as alternative entertainment makes them perfect examples of the energy of the carnival:

Let's face the music and –

Of course, we didn't know, then, how the Hazards would always upstage us. Tragedy, eternally more class than comedy. How could mere song-and-dance girls aspire so high? We were destined from birth, to be the lovely ephemera of the theatre, we'd rise and shine like birthday candles, then blow out … we would always be on the left-hand line, hoofers, thrushes, the light relief, as you might say; bring on the bears!

(pp. 58–59)

A wood outside Athens – it came up all artificial in the rushes

Gin, corsets, the Ritz and tango teas are their lives, but so is tragedy. Pretending to be Nora in the confusion of a fire during the making of the film of *A Midsummer Night's Dream*, Dora both ends up with, then loses her true love in the resulting chaos: 'To die for love runs in the family. My grandmother did it; so did my mother'(p.100).

'Kiss and tell' infamies confuse versions of Nora and Dora: 'You'll find me in his famous *Hollywood* stories. The last flame of a burned-out case, but oh, it had a glorious light!' (p.119). The girls are each represented as footnotes, marginal, vulgar, 'Vulgar as hell. The grating Cockney accent. The opportunism. The chronic insensitivity to a poet's heart' (p.119). Authors always change life to fit their art and the two walk-on parts have suffered from this in the past, but they tell their story to us, through Dora's narrative.

The depiction both of the stage settings and the actions of the 1940s film version of *A Midsummer Night's Dream* are hilarious, vulgar, excessive. Everything intends to create a sense of reality among the fantasy with: 'Daisies big as your head and white as spooks, foxgloves as tall as the tower of Pisa that chimed like bells if shook' (p.124). Everything is compared to something else, everything is artificial, everything is a construction. The flowers are stiff and cranky, the wind produced by a wind machine. Carter's text comments on the duplicitous nature of art, magic, construction.

But eventually Dora realizes the ephemerality sought in youth goes away in a desire for something more solid perhaps. Art, design and the nature of reality are all brought to mind when a play based on a dream is transferred to the Dream factory. If fantasy and reality are juxtaposed, so too are Chance and Hazard, each suggesting some version of fate or accident, a comment on whatever controls our lives and the names of Nora and Dora as opposed to their established legitimate relations, the Hazards.

> It's only a paper moon, sailing over a cardboard sea.
>
> But it wouldn't be make-believe, if you'd believe in me…
>
> (p.157)

Death does not touch the Falstaffian, larger than life Uncle Peregrine who, 'The size of a warehouse, bigger, the size of a tower block' is huge, ageless, his hair without one speck of grey, evidently untouched one jot by age (pp.206–7).

Wise Children is partly about the art of storytelling, the artifice and the fantasy of tales of media representations which magic the everyday into something weird and strange. In this novel, although there are dark sides, deaths, losses and ageing, the magic is mostly celebratory, the artifice to entertain, showing us how we construct ourselves. Nora and Dora are like the author, fixing, recording, imagining, and like the reader who needs to do the same to understand their own past origins and make sense of their lives. The novel ends with a carnivalesque gesture about continuity of life and energy, celebrating the past, establishing the present. Dora tells us:

> I am at present working on my memoirs and researching family history – see the word processor, the filing cabinet, the card indexes, right hand, left hand, right side, left side, all the dirt on everybody. What a wind! Whooping and banging all along the street, the kind of wind that blows everything topsy-turvy.
>
> Seventy-five, today, and a topsy-turvy day of wind and sunshine. The kind of wind that gets into the blood and drives you wild. Wild!
>
> (p.220)

FILM VERSIONS

The successful Neil Jordan/Angela Carter film, *The Company of Wolves*, is based on three tales, short stories from *The Bloody Chamber*, exposing latent sexuality and complicity in dominant ideology which consistently represents women as subordinate, victims. The film makes the submerged animal in man and woman more explicit. Violent, predatory, sexuality is seen both as a characteristic enabling expression of power, and a debilitating curse condemning sufferers to isolation from others. In the film, a frame tale about a modern adolescent girl is introduced, making the sexual message more explicit.

A scorned, pregnant, peasant girl exposes the lust and hypocrisy of the pretentious rich at a banquet, turning them all into the wolves they are under the surface. Their contradictions are deconstructed visually for us in the film. All the glitter of jewels and richness dissolves into furred forms and they lope off, condemned to howl around her house forever. The proximity of the wood with its narrow 'safe' path is a constant reminder of the bridled version of selves people try to maintain, when lust and the desire to oppress others lurk beneath the surface. In the film, small animals and the constant presence of the overgrown wood are foregrounded to emphasize the closeness of danger, the thinness of people's civilized veneer. Exposure to the power of latent sexuality can be dangerous. It proves fatal to (Little Red Riding Hood) Rosaleen's sister who meets a wolf and dies. Rosaleen herself meets the other kind of wolf (a werewolf), the worst sort. Granny comments 'Once you stray from the path you're lost entirely' and 'the wild beasts wait for us in the wood'. But her conventional wisdom is inappropriate. Rosaleen, meeting a handsome stranger whose eyebrows ominously meet in the middle, shows her own sexual readiness by sitting up a tree, painting her lips, and finding a baby in a stork's nest. She complies with his suggestions of a race to Granny's house. These strikingly symbolic details make even more explicit in the film what is implicit in the stories. However, audiences, expecting realism even with werewolf films, find this mixture of modes difficult to deal with. Granny's death is deliberately excessive in presentation. Her head is lopped off and falls into the milk, as the head of a werewolf lover did earlier. The film suggests their final company, rather than the female dominance on which the story ends.

One of the keys to Angela Carter's power as a writer is that she uses the myths, the forms which she wishes to deconstruct, as the very vehicles for that deconstruction. The heavy symbolism, the embellished baroque style, all lend irony, all foreground this activity so that the intention, and the achievement, become clear.

* * *SUMMARY* * *

- Angela Carter is an ironic writer and uses the myths, the forms which she wishes to deconstruct, as the vehicles for that deconstruction. So she uses fairy tale and film to show up the constrained versions of self these usually offer us.

- *The Magic Toyshop* critiques high art, myth and popular fictional representations of women though focusing on the growing up of teenage Melanie in her repressive, puppeteer toymaker Uncle Philip's house.

- *Burning your Boats* collects rewritten fairy tales and myths, and tales of domestic horror, in which Carter turns the tables on conventional tales as girls recognize their sexuality and embrace werewolves, and the tendency of the popular (male) imagination to turn women into ornaments or dolls has unpleasant repercussions.

- *Nights at the Circus* challenges both gender stereotypes and our sense of what is truth and reality with the larger-than-life, cockney, winged aerialiste Fevvers.

- *Wise Children* is a comedy, sprawling, rich and celebratory of life following the memories of music hall performer twins Dora and Nora Chance.

6 Contemporary Critical Approaches

I am all for putting new wine in old bottles, especially if the pressure of the new wine makes the old bottle explode.

(Angela Carter, 'Notes from the Front Line'
in Michelene Wandor (ed.), *On Gender and Writing*, 1983, p.69)

Although there were reviews coincident with the publication of her books and pioneering essays on Angela Carter's work in the late 1970s and early 1980s, the bulk of criticism which has established her reputation took place after her death in 1992. The first book-length study published on her was Lorna Sage's 1994 text in the Writers and their Work series, the same year as the first conference on Carter's work at York University. It is complex to review the critical response to her writing because several of her works including *Shadow Dance* (1966), *Several Perceptions* (1968) and *Love* (1971) were out of print when she first came to real critical note with the publication of *The Bloody Chamber* (1979) and they were only reissued after her death. Consequently, as Sarah Gamble notes (*The Fiction of Angela Carter: A Reader's Guide to Essential Criticism*, Icon Books, 2001), she gained her initial reputation as a feminist rewriter of fairy tales, fabulator, magical realist and, latterly, as a 'radical pornographer' (Sage, *Angela Carter*, Northcote House, 1994). Initial response to Carter's writing debated the effects of her rewriting of fairy tales and other popular cultural mythic forms, arguing she was variously effective in deliberately overturning them to critique their portrayal and perpetuation of roles of gender and power. It focused on her use of popular films, on her feminism and critique of the constraints of gender roles.

Early critics of Angela Carter's work recognize the bizarre luxuriance of her version of contemporary Bristol, London, nineteenth-century Paris, Russia, and futuristic New York. They note she has conjured a fantastic version of these worlds peopled with beautiful, destructive characters, how she rewrites fairy tale and great art to explore and expose the cultural myths which they perpetuate. Latterly, Carter's earlier works were recognized as realist in many ways, rather than fantastic or magic realist, a term applied during the 1980s to the works in print, and subsequently to all her work. Marc O'Day comments 'several of the novels actually invite readings in terms of quite traditional literary realism. True, it is a 1960s realism saturated with domesticated Gothic and psychological fantasy elements' ('Mutability is Having a Field Day: The Sixties Aura of Angela Carter's Bristol Trilogy', in Lorna Sage (ed.), *Flesh and the Mirror*, Virago, 1994).

This chapter concentrates on contemporary reviews of her work up until the 1994 conference and critical books.

Carter has identified herself as critically engaged and a materialist, but few critics pick up on this, reading her as a writer of feminist Gothic and magic realism. Gina Wisker's early essay on teaching Angela Carter's *The Magic Toyshop* ('Woman Writer, Woman Reader', *Literature Teaching Politics*, 1984 p.23) locates her work through an explicitly feminist stance:

> Angela Carter's wide grounding in material historical context, and her examination of myths of power, which encompass class and race as well as gender make her an ideal woman writer to focus on here. She states her aims and demythologies, yet refuses to construct alternative myths … Through the exploration of sexuality she undermines all ideological constrictions and lies.   (p. 23)

Many contemporary reviewers find the lavishness of Carter's text, the elaboration and description, fantasy and energies of the work overwhelming. This became particularly so by the time of the publication of *Nights at the Circus*, while of earlier works they noted the rather static nature of the excessive, ornate description, and the parodying of myths such as the monstrous Mother (of goddess and matriarchal myths) in *Passion of New Eve*, Leda and the Swan in *The Magic Toyshop* and *Nights at the Circus*.

SHADOW DANCE (1966)

Early critics of Angela Carter's first novel, *Shadow Dance* (*Honeybuzzard* in the USA) found it filled with grotesques, and with beautiful evil. Her characters, says John Bowen ('Grotesques', *New York Times*, 19 February 1967) 'live in the twilight zone'. He defines influences of Southern Gothic, an American literary Gothic written by William Faulkner, Carson McCullers, saying of Carter that, 'she has taken the whole Southern circus – mutilation and beauty and evil, hot weather and a dark luxuriance of bizarre images – and pitched her tent in Bristol. The result is a most entertaining piece of piracy, and most accomplished novel' (p.1).

THE MAGIC TOYSHOP (1967)

This novel brought Carter to the notice of a wide readership, most particularly upon its reprinting in 1980 and probably because it struck a chord with both a feminist readership fascinated with its exploration of gender stereotyping and performance, and because of its magical realism, set in a London toyshop bizarrely mixed up with mythic encounters and self-aware novelistic closure. Gina Wisker talks of teaching the text from various perspectives. 'Through utilisation of literary precedent and reader expectation, Angela Carter provides a new reading of mythology, fairytale, and our literary heritage. She exposes gender stereotyping as disseminated through popular fiction' ('Woman Writer, Woman Reader', *Literature Teaching Politics*, 1984, p.24). Paulina Palmer ('From "Coded Mannequin" to Bird Woman: Angela Carter's Magic Flight', in Sue Roe (ed.), *Women Reading Women's Writing*, Harvester, 1987) indicates interest to feminist readers because of the ways Carter uses intertextuality to analyse representations of female subordination and 'treats the relations between puppet master and puppet as symbolic of the control exerted by a patriarchal culture on women and the roles available to them'. (p.179) Carter uses male castration fears (references to Hoffmann's *The Sandman)*, while her 'analysis of the roles allocated to women in the family unit, is accompanied by a problematisation both of relations between the sexes and of heterosexual sexual practice' (Palmer, p.179). The problem is representing Melanie simultaneously as victim and autonomous individual.

HEROES AND VILLAINS (1969)

Richard Boston ('They Survived a Nuclear War', *New York Times*, 13 September 1970, p.1) identifies *Heroes and Villains*, set in a post holocaust future, as 'strange, compelling' filled with references 'to the art of the past'. Rebellious Marianne resembles both Jane Austen and D.H. Lawrence heroines. This intertextual assemblage enables Carter to construct 'a fable that discusses the roles of reason and imagination in a civilised society', recognizing that we need both, to be fully human.

THE INFERNAL DESIRE MACHINES OF DOCTOR HOFFMANN (1972) (THE WAR OF DREAMS IN THE USA)

William Hjortsberg ('Fancy Fantasy', *New York Times*, 8 September 1974) looks at the macabre, cannibalism, travelling carnival and imminent disaster 'commonplace in this world of mirages and Nebulous Time', seeing Carter's skill as detailed building on small observations. He recognizes the crucial element as fantasy and fictionality suggesting her 'ornate and intricately wrought language, although pleasingly mellifluous, often intrudes upon the narrative' (p.1), and arguing that the juxtaposition of science fictional elements such as the industry's computers and Dr Hoffman's dream transmitters sit harshly with the pure elements of the fable. But this reviewer, like others of Carter's earlier works, finds the style impenetrable at times, and legislates against such complexities for fantasy writing, 'The devious and complex nature of fantasy demands a simple style.' He compares her best writing to the grotesques of Fellini's 'Satyricon'.

THE PASSION OF NEW EVE (1977)

The Passion of New Eve was before its time in terms of postmodernist characteristics and dramatization of gender as performance, which partly explains critics' confusion when reviewing it, and the relative lack of early critical response. Peter Ackroyd ('Passion Fruit' *The*

Spectator, 26 March 1977, p.23) suggests it is 'a simple story of rape, castration and apocalypse', lurid as a future view 'That uneasy tone, perched somewhere between high seriousness and farce, unsettles the narrative as it leaps from one improbability to the next'. He sees it as grotesque, fantastic, farcical. Carter described it to Olga Kenyon as 'my most heavily plotted book, an imitation of a generically foreign novel' (*The Writer's Imagination*, University of Bradford Press, 1992, p.31) but pitched it firmly in a response to the violence and contradictions of post-Vietnam war New York where demonstrations in the streets were complemented by a kind of sterile, aesthetic cinema. 'The novel was sparked off by a visit to the USA in 1969. It was the height of the Vietnam war, with violent public demos and piles of garbage in New York streets ... it was the year of gay riots in Greenwich village ... But I wanted to make it as pleasurable as possible, I put the film stars in a real art deco house' (in Kenyon, 1992, p.31). The glass house/castle where Tristessa lives derives from Celtic mythology, the underlying Fisher King renewal myth. Carter says of Tristessa, the transvestite movie queen, 'I created this person in order to say some quite specific things about the cultural reduction of femininity', it is not merely feminist tract but 'quite a careful and elaborate discussion of femininity as a commodity, of Hollywood producing illusions as tangible commodities' (John Haffenden, 'Magical Mannerist' *Literary Review*, November 1984, p.36).

NIGHTS AT THE CIRCUS (1984)

Harriet Gilbert reviewing *Nights at the Circus* (*New Statesman*, vol. 108, 28 September 1984, p.10), finds the novel 'addictive' seeing it as about 'changes confronted and engineered by Modern Woman', endless, raising multitudes of questions. Robert Nye ('Daring Young Woman', *Guardian*, Thursday 27 September 1984, p.1) celebrates Fevver's energy and daring, arguing it is her 'coarse, uproarious, hectic, inventive, preposterous soaring through the air with the greatest of ease' which rescues the novel from being merely a feminist tract. Carolyn See

('Come on and See the Winged Lady *New York Times*, 24 February 1985) concentrates on the adventures of Jack Walser, the Californian journalist who tries to discern whether Fevvers is real or not, falls in love, and looks for magic. 'It's love that's caught him – he's stopped trying to verify whether Fevvers has a bellybutton, and longs only to be within her feathered, enchanted vicinity.' But See finds the book excessive, a 'mad mixture of Mary Poppins, Djuna Barnes *Nightwood*, Greek mythology and re-runs of the Bionic Woman'. Paul Gray (*Time*, 25 February 1985, p.87) has similar difficulties, focusing on the circus moving to St Petersburg he balks at the energies, 'Carter's florid energetic style begins turning an already complicated narrative into a three-ring extravaganza'. He spots some very obscure intertextual references: circus wife-beater Lamarck, of 'Lamarck's educated apes', references an obscure French naturalist whose version of evolution was debunked by Darwin. He recognizes a 'new fashioned love story' beneath the tale's excess and hubbub, noticing Carter's skill producing arresting images. Paulina Palmer (1987) sees women-centred ideas of liberation and rebirth enacted in the images of hatching and flight. Gina Wisker comments on the energy, philosophizing the feminist angles of the novel: '*Nights at the Circus* is largely concerned with the power of the imagination, art's ability to represent', avoiding reduction and rigidity. 'Like Fevvers, the work calls attention to itself: polemic is translated into a rococo style replete with literary and cultural echoes.' (p.29) This view is set against others' arguments that using fantasy and excess removes the novel's ability to make politicized critical comments. Wisker reads Carter alongside other postmodernists including Thomas Pynchon and John Hawkes whose philosophical basis recognizes the danger of divisive descriptions and rigid mindsets: 'The novel … exposes the false dichotomy between reason and the imagination. Woman is reified by those with reductive worldviews. The mechanical, entropic single vision which restricts or denies the imagination is indicted' ('Winged Women and Werewolves: How do we read Angela Carter?' *Ideas and Production*, 1985, p.30).

THE SADEIAN WOMAN (1979)

Ann Snitow's 1986 review essay on *Saints and Strangers* (*Nation*, 4 October 1986 p.315) also focuses on *The Sadeian Woman*, seeing Carter's 'feminist voice so unapologetic for engaging the arch enemy' de Sade and arguing that *The Sadeian Woman* was misread largely because society is divided about whether women can be as monstrous as men. The book contains opposite responses, 'an appreciation and a contempt for de Sade'. It is 'shameless and aggressive', a problematic stance for a woman who would critique male culture, 'consciously ironic about all phallic authority'. As an invention and counter-fiction to de Sade's intellectual work, it shows Carter's love/hate relationship to rules, and her fascination with the ostensible liberty offered by de Sade.

THE BLOODY CHAMBER (1979)

Critics commenting on *The Bloody Chamber*, Carter's first collection of short stories, debated her fascination with 'sadistic power and masochistic sacrifice' characterizing the tales as macabre like her novels. Alan Friedman ('Pleasure and Pain' *Theatre Directory*, 17 February 1980, p.2) criticizes Carter's characteristic florid style: 'Perhaps there are thousands of readers ready for the cutesy mannerisms and comical overwriting, the whipped passion as full of cold air as whipped butter' in her fairy tales and horror tales. 'Most of these stories have the kind of cloying cleverness we associate with precious writers' although the collection improves, he argues: 'several of the last stories are jewels, direct and intense'. Interestingly, although it took a while for Carter to develop the same kind of readership in the USA as the UK, there were thousands of readers ready for her fresh, overwhelming style and her new vision.

Patricia Duncker ('Reimagining the Fairytales: Angela Carter's "Bloody Chambers", *Literature and History*, vol 10:1, Spring, 1984) argues from a feminist angle that Carter falls foul of the trap of the fairy tales, fixing the form to its purpose, as the vehicle of ideology. In rewriting fairy tales, she suggests, Carter continues to create characters defined by their roles. A 'bolder hand' is necessary as the work otherwise 'reproduces rather than alters, the original deeply rigidly sexist psychology of the erotic' (p.12). Women become merely the mirror image of male predatoriness. The result is collusion with, not an exposé of, pornographic elements underwriting fairy tales.

Joyce Carol Oates ('Comedy as Tragedy that happens to Other People', *New York Times*, 19 January 1992, p.1) notes of *The Bloody Chamber* that it has had the greatest effect in the USA and 'is distinguished by bold' language and ornate, often bloody imagery; its aesthetic agenda a wilful appropriation of the old tales and legends of patriarchal world. Oates argues the tales actively, politically rejecting cultural stereotypes.

BLACK VENUS (1985) *(SAINTS AND STRANGERS)* IN THE USA

'Everyday life among the mythic classes' is how Lorna Sage describes the stories in this volume ('Breaking the Spell of the Past', *Times Literary Supplement*, 18 October 1985, p.1169) although where Jeanne Duvalle, Baudelaire's mistress and Lizzie Borden the axe murderess are concerned, this is hardly everyday experience. Carter, Sage notes, takes 'the people out of the museum, sets them in motion, subjects them to surmise'. Duvalle is seen lighting cheroots with Baudelaire's manuscripts, not dreaming of exotic shores, and surviving in a rich if rather pox-ridden old age having inherited both his illness and his wealth. Elsewhere, 'Overture and Incidental music of *A Midsummer Night's Dream*' depicts the fantasy figures as real, giving fairies bad colds. Charles Newman ('A Maker of Magic Souffle', *New York Times*, 7 September 1986) argues against the marketing of Carter as 'eccentric English author, a fabulist and a feminist' (p.1) seeing hers as a unique voice 'intensely literary without being pretentious, deep without being difficult, indifferent to formula without being 'experimental', and funny without being superficial or cruel' (p.1). He looks past 'the Cabinet of Edgar Allen Poe', arguing Carter evokes 'the tissue of infinite regret and regress upon which Poe's poetry, never mentioned, was written' capturing his bizarre life, including the unfortunate marriage to the corpse-like Virginia. Newman notices psychological processes appearing in 'Peter and the Wolf' suggesting 'the drama lies frequently in the helplessness of the historical figure as his personal experience becomes mythologized' (p.2). In the same vein, when Herbert Mitgang phone-interviews Carter, she questions the label magic realism, arguing 'It's more realism than not ... I can't define it until after it's done except that it's definitely fiction, it's more in the genre of Latin American writers like Garcia Marquez and Borges, Borges was by far my most important influence, I first read him in 1969' (p.2). Ann Snitow (*Nation,* 4 October 1986, p.315) recognizes Carter was only gradually appreciated by American readers, 'almost as if American publishers see her as a wine that won't travel well'. In considering the range of her short stories, and her indulgence in fairytales, Snitow prompts us to stick with the text until Carter reveals her secrets. 'By telling fairy tales, she chooses a fictional world' conforming to a certain economy of roles: 'patterns determine that little girls will run away and big wolves give chase. But the unconscious always erupts in a Carter story: Beauty falls in love with the beast as a beast; she doesn't want a prince. Neither freedom nor pleasure is rational or safe though, ironically both have their own determining strictures'.

WISE CHILDREN (1991)

Carole Angier ('Song and Dance', *New Statesman*, vol. 4: 155, 14 June 1991) sets the record straight about Carter's variety, admitting she expected a dark and difficult writer, intellectual, feminist, interested in the sinister and supernatural. Instead, *Wise Children* is extravagant, energetic, fun, filled with the magical which is plainly real, that of the drama and the screen. Angier captures the Shakespearean quality of this last work, its use of twinning, coincidence and the happy ending. Salman Rushdie paid tribute to her storytelling skills ('Angela Carter, 1940–1992: A Very Good Wizard, a Very Dear Friend', *New York Times Book Review,* 8 March 1992, p.5) calling *Wise Children* her finest novel, 'in it, we hear the full range of her off-the-page, real-life voice, the novel is written with her unique brand of deadly cheeriness. It cackles gaily as it impales the century upon its jokes'. The text resurrects the clanging dustbin lid voice and style of Fevvers from the earlier *Nights at the Circus*. Ann Snitow (*Nation*, 20 April 1992, p.526), following Carter's death, says she expected the usual occasions, 'eccentric household dinners, carnivals, magic shows, birthday parties that get out of control'. Instead she found 'a complex philosophical work on the ambiguity of biological ties, on the family romance, in the theatre generally (Shakespearean in particular) and above all, on pleasure'. Snitow explores and celebrates the energies and fun of the novel, the left-hand, wrong side of the tracks, memories from the dubious Dora.

* * *SUMMARY* * *

● Some critics found her fairy tales radical critiques, others argued they confirmed the status quo.

● Her embellished style, twinning, irony, paradoxical and controversial use of pornography and de Sade, her comedy, all produced varied responses – some critical, some supportive.

7 Modern Critical Approaches

Be advised ... this writer is no meat-and-potatoes hack; she is a rocket, a Catherine Wheel.

(Salman Rushdie, introduction to *Burning your Boats*)

The main critical work and all book-length studies of Carter's writing followed her death in 1992, beginning with Lorna Sage's two ground-breaking publications in 1994, *Angela Carter* (Northcote House) and the collection *Flesh and the Mirror* (Virago). Following this, further essays and books have appeared by Linden Peach, Aidan Day, Bristow and Broughton, Sarah Gamble and Alison Easton among others, and there have been many critical revisitings of her earlier work, particularly the Bristol Trilogy (so named by Marc O'Day), incorporating *Shadowdance*, *Several Perceptions* and *Love*, which (with the exception of *Love*, republished earlier) were republished in the 1990s.

FEMINIST DEBATES

'Truly it felt like year one' said Carter (*Shaking a Leg: Journalism and Writings, The Collected Angela Carter*, ed. Jennifer Uglow, Chatto and Windus, 1997, p.37), exhilarated by the potential for reconfigurations of gender positions and women's sexual freedoms offered in the 1960s with the advent of second-wave feminism. However, reception of her work as a feminist has not always been so straightforwardly celebratory.

Carter is nothing if not paradoxical and response to her work is also filled with paradox. The early *Shadow Dance* and *Several Perceptions* were criticized for their use of a male narrator and the brutality dealt to women. Sarah Gamble (*Angela Carter: Writing from the Front Line*, Edinburgh University Press, 1997, pp.54–5) indicts the 'camp burlesque' of *Shadow Dance* for offering a 'nasty shock' to those considering Carter a feminist. Freedom seems only available to men and 'the treatment meted out to Ghislaine, make(s) some kind of moral response to the text on the part of the reader unavoidable'. At this period in her career, Carter herself says she 'didn't see the point of feminism' (Susannah Clapp, 'On Madness, Men and Fairytales', *Independent on Sunday*, 9 June 1991, p.26) but she also acknowledges its influence in all she does: 'I don't think I'd be the person I am if it weren't for the women's movement in the Sixties' (in interview with John Mortimer, 'The Stylish Prime of Miss Carter', *Sunday Times*, 24 January 1982, p.36).

Feminist attacks largely critique use of sadistic male protagonists in the early fiction and Carter's celebration of the radical pornographer de Sade in *The Sadeian Woman*. Carter's argument is that for all his violence, nonetheless (and in the right contexts presumably), 'de Sade put pornography in the service of women' (*The Sadeian Woman*, p .51), something that anti-pornographers such as Andrea Dworkin would argue was impossible. Susanne Kappeler (*The Pornography of Representation*, Cambridge: Poling Press, 1986) accuses Carter of validating the pornographic while Linda Williams (*Hard Core*, London: Pandora, 1990) sees her work as radical and anti-censorship, pro the exercising of women's sexual liberties.

Other critics have explored Carter's representation of men, notably Paul Magrs ('Boys Keep Swinging', Bristow and Broughton eds.1996), who recognizes how Carter appoints her executioners, puppet masters and patriarchs. They have, like Uncle Philip in *The Magic Toyshop*, 'an overwhelming male ego in a toyboxful of dressing-up clothes' (p.189). Carter recognizes their inability to ironize their own performances. They remain bullies who treat women as objects and puppets. Honeybuzzard's male beauty in *Shadow Dance* and the husband in 'The Bloody Chamber' are each intent on mutilating their women. Carter has little space for new men, but she does develop the character of the blind piano-tuner in 'The Bloody Chamber' and Walser in *Nights at the Circus*. 'Whether he knows it or not, the moment he steps into the boudoir of the music-hall starlet he is set on a course of self-reconstruction from a starting point of privilege' (Magrs, 1996, p.184). In Jean Wyatt's 'The Violence of Gendering: Castration Images in Angela Carter's *The Magic Toyshop*, *The Passion of New Eve* and 'Peter and the Wolf' (*New Casebooks*, ed. Alison Easton, Macmillan, 2000), Carter is seen as answering Freud's depiction of woman as castrated, by replacing and celebrating an image of active female sexuality, offering 'an alternative as well as a critique of patriarchal sexual relations' in *The Magic Toyshop* (Easton, 200, p.72).

GENDER PLAY AND PERFORMANCE

Ground-breaking discussions of gender performances appear in *The Passion of New Eve*, latterly identified as a radical feminist text although Carter herself indicated in interview that she deliberately wrote it as a critique of the constructions and representations of femininity produced by the Hollywood movie industry. Heather L Johnson ('Unexpected Geometries: Transgressive Symbolism and the Transsexual Subject in Angela Carter's *The Passion of New Eve*, Bristow and Broughton, eds, 1997, p.167) recognizes it as a groundbreaking work: 'Her novel seems to pre-empt, by nearly two decades, recent developments in the discipline of gender studies such as in the intersection of gender theory and transsexual autobiography' and 'looks at the act of passing, the drag queen's experiences' of both Evelyn and Tristessa. 'In assuming the exaggerated shape of the drag queen, Tristessa's own subjectivity is triply mediated by the role of starlet, the fictional heroines she plays, and the cinema screen itself'. In the same volume, Paulina Palmer ('Gender as Performance in the Fiction of Angela Carter' in Bristow and Broughton, eds, 1997, p.51) relates Carter and Atwood's work to that of Judith Butler. A key theorist in the context of gender as performance, Butler argues that gender is not essential but constituted through a set of 'discursively constrained performative acts that produce the body through and within the categories of sex' (*Gender Trouble: Feminism and the Subversion of Identity*, Routledge, 1990, p.x). Based on this set of theories, Butler explores two positions of femininity which Palmer finds reflected in Carter's work 'femininity as entrapment' and 'femininity as self-invention and role-mobilization' (Palmer, in Bristow and Broughton, p.31). Similarly Mary Russo ('Revamping Spectacle' in Easton (ed.), 2000, p.155) replays the stereotypical male image of woman as aerialist, a role constructed by men, recognizing that Carter deliberately gives foster mother Lizzie the power to create and nurture Fevvers's flight and her identity in *Nights at the Circus*. Carter's work is seen by Palmer as an example of exploration of the ambivalent nature of the grotesque female body in relation to the 'body politic'; (ibid.) of masquerade.

MAGIC REALISM – CARTER AND STYLE

By her own admissions, Carter was influenced greatly by the Latin American magic realists Garcia Marquez and Borges, and her identification with magical realism to some extent overshadowed appropriate critical recognition for the ways in which she engages with political and cultural issues. This is so because until the late 1990s, the modes which magical realism related to or made use of most readily, those of fantasy and surrealism, were considered by many critics to be at odds with any such engaged comment, but Carter is always engaged. Latterly, we are more aware that engagement is not the exclusive property of realism and mimesis/copying the world.

Nights at the Circus is the high point in Carter's magic realism, largely because at its centre is the bird woman Fevvers herself, a mix of the earthily real cockney and the magical fantastic embodiment of women's freedom, a winged woman seen as 'a glorious enchantment', a 'spellbinding achievement' (Gillian Greenwod, 'Flying Circus' *Literary Review* October, 1984, p.43). The novel uses feminist images of flying and celebration, and Bakhtinian images of the grotesque woman's body in a celebratory manner. 'The most powerful image of liberation and transformation in the novel is Fevvers herself and her magnificent wings' (Paulina Palmer's 'From Coded Mannequin to Bird Woman: Angela Carter's Magic Flight', in Sue Roe (ed.), *Women Reading Women's Writing*, Harvester, 1987, pp.197–200).

HORROR AND THE GOTHIC

Carter has also been seen critically as part of the new wave of contemporary women writers of the Gothic for her use of paradox, irony, myth, fairy tale and horror tropes to critique the contemporary world. One of her favourite subjects for Gothic and horror writing is the gendered construction and representations of power which render woman as automata, puppets and femmes fatale. Carter's rewriting of certain fairy tales and horror scenarios, including the female vampire and the werewolf, celebrate sexuality in 'The Company of Wolves' where the young girl jumps into bed with the wolf, or critique family tyrannies and patriarchal power in *The Magic Toyshop* as explored in Gina Wisker's essays on Carter's horror (in *Creepers*, London: Pluto Press 1994, and *Gothic Horror*, Houndmills: Macmillan 1998).

MANNERISM AND ENGAGEMENT

'Mannerist' is the style Carter preferred rather than magic realist (interview with Angela Carter in John Haffenden's *Novelists in Interview*, Methuen, 1985, p.81). Bristow and Broughton comment: 'Carter's early decision to become a "mannerist" sometimes appeared eccentric in a writer whose radical political interests were both feminist and socialist. Undeniably, her "mannerist" method stood in serious opposition to the austerity of social realism, the traditional genre for representing the grinding oppression of women, workers and minorities' (Introduction, Joseph Bristow and Trev Lynn Broughton (eds.), *The Infernal Desires of Angela Carter*, Blackwell, 1997, p.6). This collection of essays looks mainly at Carter's treatment of gender and performance, gender roles, and re-engagement with cultural and political issues through the means of a feminist-inspired fantastic, magical realism.

One debate around her use of elaborate style and focus upon feminist and populist concerns, centres on some members of the literary establishment's insistence that you cannot and should not combine literary elegance and pop art. Of course, Carter can and does, irritating many, such as John Bayley, writing two months after her death: 'Angela Carter is good at having it both ways, dressing up pop art in academic gear and presenting crude aspects of modern living in a satirically elegant style' which he feels is problematic because 'if there is a common factor in the elusive category of the postmodern style, it is political correctness' ('Fighting for the Crown', *New York Review of Books*, 23 April 1992, p.10). Hermione Lee ('A Room of One's Own, or a Bloody Chamber? Angela Carter's Political Correctness', in Sage (ed.), *Flesh and the Mirror*, Virago, 1994) sees Bayley as constructing an arch feminist here and refutes the idea that Carter is in collusion with political correctness, a stance which would ridicule her engagement with the political as a fad or a deliberate, paltry response. Such criticism deliberately maligned her in the USA where her work was then less well known and made her sound 'rigid and intolerant' (p.313) because labelled as politically correct and feminist. Her work is more complex. Lee, looking at Carter's readings and borrowings, finds her in alignment with the working-class voice and deliberate engagement with everyday people. Merja Makinen identifies Carter's active subversion ('Angela Carter's "The Bloody Chamber" and the Decolonisation of Feminine Sexuality', *Feminist Review*, vol. 42, Autumn, 1992, pp.2–3, reprinted in Easton (ed.), 2000) questioning the rather comforting image of Carter as a white witch built on Margaret Atwood's memorial in the *Observer*, which opens with Carter's 'intelligence and kindness' constructing her as a 'mythical, fairytale white witch' someone who looked and acted like the Fairy Godmother. She seemed always on the verge of producing 'some talisman, some magic token'. Sage's obituary in the *Guardian* talks of her 'powers of enchantment and hilarity, her generous inventiveness'. Makinin points out this is too simple, mythologizing Carter reduces the challenge of her problematic treatment of pornography and sexuality.

Carter is a subversive writer because she ironizes and exposes the contradictions of oppressive constructions whether gender, the colonial or of relationships in general. The absurdities carried out in the name of patriarchy are favourites, but not everyone in the literary establishment can either appreciate or applaud this. Neither can they cope with the eclectic nature of her style which litters relevant references intertextually from popular Hollywood film, myth, Shakespeare, the modernists, Freud and de Sade, among others.

FANTASY, CARNIVAL AND SOCIAL CRITIQUE

Aidan Day also recognizes Carter's political engagement, identifying her as a writer with designs upon her readers (*The Rational Glass*, Manchester University Press, p.215). Considering *Wise Children*, he notes, 'There are hints, in the variety and multiplicity of life on the streets of her beloved London and elsewhere, that an alternative English cultural model of reciprocity, tolerance and equality may be in the making, as Carter would have wished it'. It is a positive, celebratory text. Day's full-length study takes a political, philosophical reading, relating her realism and fantasy to cultural criticism. Linden Peach's well-written study of Carter's work concentrates in the main on her celebration of the development of the novel, recognizing her social engagement 'not to be confused with any social realism' as essentially ludic, characterized by linguistic play. Even the more 'realistic' early texts are parodic, allusive and, sometimes, exclusive. Such artistic innovation has been regarded by social realist Marxist critics and writers as too decadent, introverted and bourgeois: non-realistic fiction 'distances or alienates us so we are disturbed, puzzled, confused and possibly very critical of what we are reading' (Linden Peach, *Angela Carter*, Macmillan,1998, p.6). Carter uses alienating techniques and the fantastic but is always socially and culturally engaged. Punter also investigates Carter's use of the carnivalesque, recognizing that this derives more from the energies of Shakespeare than Bakhtin and is a theme rather than a writing position. The theatre in Carter is a subversive, illegitimate power able to challenge the gendered intellectual and political status quo. Peach considers how Carter explores 'different sites of the illegitimate power associated with the theatre, the carnivalesque, the masque, the brothel' and social margins (ibid. p.145). Her work refuses all orthodoxies, relates fantasy and the theatre, spectacle and vaudeville but like Beckett she 'tried to develop a novel form that ... would accommodate contradiction and confusion' while remaining art (ibid., p. 170). Peach sees her as engaged and revolutionary, paradoxical and theatrical.

* * * SUMMARY * * *

● Angela Carter began in the 1990s to be fully appreciated as a key contemporary postmodernist woman writer able to explore and critique historically, culturally and politically engaged issues.

● She investigates and exposes relations and constructions of gender and power.

● Her use of magic realism, the fantastic, the comic and popular fictional genres such as science fiction/utopian and romantic fiction are playful, entertaining and socially/politically engaged.

● Carter's work is seen as postmodernist in relating to the use of intertextuality, philosophical engagement, the fantastic, reinterpretation of established myths, popular versions and popular cultural history.

● She is a wonderfully entertaining storyteller.

8 Where to Next?

There are a number of Angela Carter short stories and novels to read such as her earlier *Shadow Dance, Love* and *Several Perceptions*. There are also other writers who write rather like her, such as contemporaries Fay Weldon, Sarah Maitland, Emma Tennant, Margaret Atwood and Michele Roberts, Gothic writers, 'magic realists,' and Latin American writers, for example Gabriel Garcia Marquez, Carlos Fuentes, Jorge Luis Borges and Isabel Allende. Other postmodernists such as Martin Amis and Ian McEwan critique their times or, as Julian Barnes and Pat Barker, cast doubts on absolute reality, revealing historical constructions. Interesting also are writers concerned with celebration, the carnivalesque. You could read those who influenced Carter such as Baudelaire, the Jacobean revenge tragedy dramatists Webster, Tourneur and Shakespeare of course, whose influences are noticeable in *Wise Children*. Look, too, at modernist poets including W.B. Yeats and T.S. Eliot whose work she echoes, also Dickens for grim nineteenth- century settings and Victorian patriarchal overtones in, for instance, *The Magic Toyshop*.

Angela Carter wrote a number of interesting essays and short stories exploring and discussing representations of gendered relationships, constructions of what is considered feminine, and critiques of the works of other writers such as Edgar Allen Poe. Her work has been turned into two films, *The Magic Toyshop* and *The Company of Wolves*, worth watching as they capture the artifice and the danger, the sense of magic in her work. A very interesting *Omnibus* programme, *The Curious Room*, followed her death in 1992. There are many websites to visit, and *The Magic Toyshop* has recently (2001) been turned into a successful play by Bryony Lavery.

SHADOW DANCE (1966)

Angela Carter's first published novel, the dramatically rather static *Shadow Dance* evokes the pretentiousness and danger of the 1960s in Bohemian Bristol, where charismatic and violent Honeybuzzard manipulates the lives of others around him, disfiguring the beautiful Ghislaine and drawing second-hand art dealer Morris into his circle. Clothing and representation are uppermost in the novel, an early piece of women's horror writing, staged, nasty, set in pubs and shops, cellars and flats. It opens with the startling return of disfigured beauty Ghislaine, whose new face-length scar shocks ex-lover Morris.

HEROES AND VILLAINS (1969)

In a post-holocaust world of white towers and mutant tribes, Marianne runs away from her father, joining a tribe of tattooed barbarians led by Donally, ex-professor and shaman. This is a novel about alienation, otherness and cruelty. Jewel, who rapes Marianne, is abused by Donally and Marianne ends up deciding to rule the tribe as a matriarch, replacing Donally, the patriarch.

ESSAYS

Angela Carter's essays are mostly collected in *Nothing Sacred, Expletives Deleted* and *Shaking a Leg*. In some of these we see her working out ideas about gender as performance, the pantomime excess of our relationships with each other which traverse the human and animal boundary, the tragic and comic, and which provide self-aware entertainment. This influences *Wise Children* and the carnivalesque moments throughout her work, most explicitly in *Nights at the Circus*. Other essays explore the influence of America, and of other writers, such as D.H. Lawrence (whom she depicts as a closet queen because of his interest in clothing in *Women In Love*) and Edgar Allen Poe. Carter also writes of Hollywood, a great influence because of the constructedness, the performativity of the representation of gendered roles of relationships, love and power, and its questioning of reality and identity. Essays and reviews deal with male and female beauty, advertisements, pornography, William Burroughs, Hanif Kureishi, food, fashion, birth and madness. Carter says the American section of the book recognizes that Hollywood had colonized the imagination of the entire world and was turning us all into Americans, while of the gender section 'she is answering back' because she was a woman and 'men thought they had the right to tell me how to feel but then I stopped listening to them and tried to forge it out for myself' (p.5).

THE CURIOUS ROOM: PLAYS, FILM SCRIPTS AND AN OPERA (1996)

This selection of Angela Carter's dramatic works encompasses the radio plays in *Come Unto These Yellow Sands* (1985). The editor, Susannah Clapp, tells of Carter revealing the enormous influence the 1930s mirror- and chandelier-filled Granada Theatre, Tooting, had on her in her youth. It was grandiose, artificial and within it fantasy reigned making her aware that everything was performance and construction. Several of the plays in this selection have never been dramatized and were discovered after Carter's death, in her study, while others such as *Vampirella*, a version of 'The Lady in the House of Love', have been broadcast. *Come Unto These Yellow Sands* focuses on the life of the painter of fairies, Richard Dadd, who killed his father, a theme returning in the two short stories about Lizzie Borden, 'The Fall River Axe Murders' and 'Lizzie's Tigers'. Carter also dramatizes Virginia Woolf's novel of androgyny, *Orlando* (as yet unstaged).

OTHER WRITERS TO READ
Fay Weldon

Another writer critiquing constrained roles for, and representations of, women using myth, magic and humour, is Fay Weldon whose *The Life and Loves of a She Devil* focuses on one woman's rebellion against the constraints of domesticity and the lies of romantic fictions affecting women's sense of purpose and their own narratives. Weldon's novels use magic and humour to critique women's constrained lives and the cultural myths which ensure this constraint, enabling women to challenge and move somewhat beyond these constraints even if they conform in recognizing love and relationships as their real goal. In *Growing Rich*, three Fenland girls are doomed to dead-end jobs. However, the Devil's henchman, Driver, cruises past in his Black BMW and offers one of the girls, Carmen, everything she might desire, if she will be the consort of Sir Bernard Bellamy, local magnate, whose soul Driver seeks to own. Carmen outwits him. Fay Weldon's work, like

Carter's and Atwood's, demythologizes the myths which constrain women's representations.

Margaret Atwood

In *The Handmaid's Tale*, Atwood envisages a future where women's reproductive abilities enslave them as handmaids. In *The Edible Woman*, the protagonist, Marion, decides she does not want to be constructed and consumed by her partner. In *Alias Grace*, and *The Blind Assassin*, Atwood deals with re-revitalizing periods of history, casting a critical light upon ways in which we reconstruct and perpetuate versions of the past. In so doing, she interrogates different social forms of testimony, documentary and historical records, the official forms of history showing they provide a very partial interpretation. All forms of record are interpretations.

Pat Barker

Pat Barker's work was encouraged by Angela Carter, who taught her in a writing class. It initially concentrated on the lives of working-class women in the North of England, Preston. *Union Street* is a series of short stories building into a novel, considering women in a single street, their ages ranging from a young girl to an old woman, their lives encompassing a series of hardships, abusive or absent partners, rape, abortion, prostitution, penury and some sisterhood and support. Harsh lives of similar women are also explored in *Blow the House Down* and *The Century's Daughter*.

With her *Regeneration* trilogy, however, Barker moved into new territory, that of rewriting history from different points of view. *Regeneration*, *The Eye in the Door* and *The Ghost Road* are versions of rewritten history, making readers aware of the constructedness and gendered nature of history itself.

Edgar Allen Poe

Nineteenth-century American Gothic writer Edgar Allan Poe wrote the first murder mysteries 'Murders in the Rue Morgue' and several early horror stories including 'The Pit and the Pendulum' and 'The Masque of the Red Death'. Poe's stories are carefully, tightly wrought, have an atmosphere of threat and plumb the fears and problems of the human psyche. Pre-Jung and Freud, Poe understood terrors of being buried alive, the threat to the sense of domestic stability and the familiar in 'The Fall of the House of Usher', the terrors of crossing boundaries between life and death as in 'Ligeia' where a dead wife returns. Poe's fears and problems deeply influenced Carter, as did his Gothic imagery.

Latin American Writers

Gabriel Garcia Marquez and others use magic realism, mixing the historical, factual, the seeming real, with the magical, fantastical in order to represent the minds and imagination, nightmares and dreams of people, using the same tone for each. Marquez's *One Hundred Years of Solitude*, follows a single family in South America over 100 years. Kept together by a strong woman, Ursula (living over 100 years) the family experience levitation, massacres, visits from gypsies with magic carpets and invading multinationals taking over banana plantations. Marquez, like Carter, is influenced by the philosophical, paradoxical Borges, and influences Isabelle Allende who also writes family narrative, and mixes the magical and the historical much as Carter does in *Wise Children* and her short stories.

Jane Austen, and Charlotte, Emily and Anne Brönte

Carter's fascination with the lives of women throughout the ages can be traced back to earlier women writers such as the Bröntes, Austen, their Gothic passions and social conformity. Both Austen and the Bröntes deal with heightened imagination, irony, paradox and contradiction, on which Carter is also an expert.

* * *SUMMARY* * *

- Read more by Angela Carter.

- Watch the film *The Company of Wolves* directed by Neil Jordan, (1984), and *The Magic Toyshop* (1984).

- Read work by other contemporary and postmodernist writers, other writers concerned with sexuality, relationships, ironizing forms and expressions, dealing in black humour such as Margaret Atwood, Ian McEwan and Fay Weldon.

Chronology of Major Works

1966 Her first novel *Shadow Dance*
1966 A collection of poems 'Five Quiet Shouters' is printed in Poet and Printer
1966 'Unicorn' her second collection of poems is published
1967 *The Magic Toyshop*
1968 *Several Perceptions*
1969 *Heroes and Villains*
1971 *Love*
1972 *The Infernal Desire Machines of Doctor Hoffman*
1974 First collection of short stories, *Fireworks*
1977 *The Passion of New Eve*
1979 Her second collection of short stories *The Bloody Chamber*
1979 The children's work *Martin Leman's Comic and Curious Cats*
1979 Translates *The Fairy Tales of Charles Perrault*
1979 *The Sadeian Woman: An Exercise in Cultural History* and *The Bloody Chamber*
1982 First collection of essays 'Nothing Sacred'
1982 *Moonshadow* (with J. Todd)
1984 *Nights at the Circus*
1984 *Screenplay: The Company of Wolves,* film directed by Neil Jordan – Freudian version of 'little red riding hood', based on the premise that a wolf may not be what he seems
1985 *Black Venus*
1985 *Come Unto These Yellow Sands* (plays)
1986 *Saints and Strangers*
1986 Edit *Wayward Girls and Wicked Women*
1991 *Wise Children*
1991 *Sleeping Beauty and Other Favourite Fairytales*
1992 *Expletives Deleted: Selected Writings*
1990 Edit *The Virago Book of Fairy Tales*
1992 Ed *The Second Virago Book of Fairy Tales*
1993 *American Ghosts and Old World Wonders*
1995 *Burning your Boats: Collected Stories*
1996 *The Curious Room: Plays, Film Scripts and an Opera,* introduction by Susannah Clapp, edited by Mark Bell
1997 *Shaking a Leg: Collected Writings,* edited by J. Uglow

GLOSSARY

Carnival The critical term carnival was coined by Mikhail Bakhtin, who recognized that in medieval and Renaissance days, ordinary people would, on certain days of the year, particularly Twelfth Night and midsummer, turn the tables, mock the rich, play, celebrate and have fun. Bakhtin labelled these activities and other critical subversive, energetic critiques as 'carnival', now a term used by many contemporary writers, creative and critical, to identify reactions against repression, the celebratory energies of alternative ways of living, something of a lively riotous time.

Gothic and contemporary feminist Gothic Gothic is a term linked to Gothic architecture, soaring turrets, dungeons, winding stairs, and buildings. But in literary terms the Gothic is usually seen to begin with Horace Walpole's *Castle of Otranto* and Anne Radcliffe's *Mysteries of Udolpho*. It forms a major influence in much nineteenth-century writing, particularly romantic tales which also involve incarceration, threats, virginity and tyrannical, powerful men. Gothic also was used as a vehicle for social critique. Ostensibly secure social situations – families, relationships, homes – are seen as founded on doubt and deception,

their contradictions a leak through in imagery of gap and breaks, mirrors and contradictions. In conventional nineteenth-century Gothic, usually such exposés of contradiction lead to a final, secure ending with order restored. In contemporary feminist Gothic, the very kind of security and stability is cast in doubt, seen as reinforcing an order more supportive of dominant middle-class white masculinist beliefs and behaviours, and not so generously inclined towards the needs and lives of women. So some contemporary Gothic writers, such as Michele Roberts and Angela Carter, refuse neat endings and the restoration of order.

Intertextuality Used by artists and writers of all kinds, particularly twentieth- and twenty-first century writers, intertextuality is the deliberate referencing, direct use of, mingling into a work of other works by other artists and writers, suggesting their influence, and contradictions or parallels with their arguments and ideas.

Magic realism Originating in the works of Latin American writers such as Gabriel Garcia Marquez 1960s onwards, magic realism is a form of writing combining both the factual or realistic, and the magical, imaginative and supernatural. Authors show people's imaginative, lived feelings *and* what they actually say and do. It enables writers to show paradox, contradictions. Great twentieth- century magic realists include Angela Carter and Toni Morrison.

Other   A critical term used in much post-colonial and horror writing, it suggests the emphasis of difference, foreignness, leading to prejudice and oppression.

Oxymoron   A conjunction of contradictions, of opposites, such as 'beautiful decay' or 'exquisite corpse' and it shows up contradictions, what is hidden.

Pre-Raphaelite   The pre-Raphaelite Brotherhood was a group of mid-nineteenth-century writers and artists, including Dante Gabriel Rossetti and Holman Hunt. They revived the very realistic styles of painting that were popular before the work of the Renaissance painter Raphael, and did so to tell stories, retell myths and comment socially on everything from moral laxity to emigration.

Patriarchy   This literally means the law of the father, but has been taken to suggest legitimized, enforced, male dominated *oppression*. Many feminist thinkers such as writer Virginia Woolf, or French feminist theorist Hélène Cixous, have written against the damage that patriarchal power has done to women, and to the

vulnerable (children, people from other countries, the poor), subordinating and silencing them. It is important to note that criticizing patriarchy is not a criticism of men as such but of oppressive power enabled by a damaging male dominance.

Second wave feminism   Second-wave feminism, or the Women's Movement, started in the late 1960s with demands for equal rights and equal pay. Some writers and thinkers rediscovered goddess myths, imagining matriarchal communities which would refuse war and violence (seen as largely male activities). 'Take back the night' marches insisted that women should be free to live their own lives, not preyed on by the violence of men in the night streets. The movement, articulated in the 1970s texts such as Germaine Greer's *The Female Eunuch* and Kate Millet's *Sexual Politics*, heralded a sexual revolution and led to changes in the material, legal and social situation of many women.

FURTHER READING

Angela Carter websites:

http://www.centerforbokculture.org/interviews/interview_carter.html
http://www.kirjasto.sci.fi/acarter.htm

Bristow, J., and Broughton, T.L. (eds.), *The Infernal Desires of Angela Carter: Fiction, Femininity, Feminism* (Oxford : Blackwell, 1997).

Day, A., *Angela Carter: The Rational Glass* (Manchester: Manchester University Press, 1998).

Gamble, S. *Angela Carter: Writing from the Front Line* (Edinburgh: Edinburgh University Press, 1997).

Haffenden, J., *Novelists in Interview,* (London: Methuen, 1985).

Palmer, P. 'From "Coded Mannequin" to Bird Woman: Angela Carter's Magic Flight', in Sue Roe (ed.), *Women Reading Women's Writing,* (London: Harvester, 1987).

Peach, L. *Angela Carter,* (Houndmills: Macmillan, 1999).

Sage, L. *Angela Carter,* (Plymouth: Northcote House, 1994).

Sage, L. (ed.), *Flesh and the Mirror: Essays on the Art of Angela Carter* (London: Virago, 1994).

Wisker, G. 'Angela Carter's horror', in C. Bloom (ed.), *Gothic Horror* (London: Macmillan, 1999).

Wisker, G. 'Woman Writer, Woman Reader', *Literature Teaching Politics* (Vol. 3, 1984 pp.18–32).

Wisker, G. 'Winged Women and Werewolves: How Do We Read Angela Carter?', *Ideas and Production* (Vol. 7, 1985 pp.26–35).

INDEX